An Invitation into
Great Intimacy with the Father

SUMMONED
out of
DARKNESS

MB BUSCH

FOREWORD BY JOAN HUNTER

Summoned Out of Darkness

An Invitation into Great Intimacy with the Father

© MB Busch 2019

Note: Author has chosen to capitalize all pronouns that refer to God, Jesus and Holy Spirit, regardless of the cited Bible version's style.

ISBN: 978-0-578-50000-3

hohministries.org

ROYALTY PRESS

SUMMONED
out of
DARKNESS

ENDORSEMENTS

Come along with MB as she takes you on a journey from death to life. A journey where God turns ashes into beauty. The raw truth of this book leaves the reader wanting to know more. How does someone go from alcoholism, drug addiction, and bulimia, to an abundant life of joy, beauty, love, and laughter? How can we all be set free from "prisons" in our lives?

Join MB as she pours out her heart in this candid book, and you'll be amazed at the power of God. Oh, how He loves to turn messes into miracles!

PAULETTE REED

PAULETTE REED MINISTRIES

MB is shining a light on the hidden battles many face in her book *Summoned Out of Darkness*. Find hope, feel the Father's love for you, and begin taking steps in the direction of your destiny.

CHARITY BRADSHAW

AUTHOR | SPEAKER

PRESIDENT OF LIFEWISE BOOKS

I have seen first-hand how God has and is working in MB's life to release her destiny. *Summoned Out of Darkness* shares MB's story of recovery, redemption, and release into God's gifting. Her story will give you hope and encouragement for the challenges you face in life and help uncover the unique gifting only you have. Enjoy!

GARY BORGENDALE

LOCAL MINISTRY DIRECTOR

SALEM MEDIA GROUP – MINNEAPOLIS

What an inspiration MB is to her family and friends as she lives a radically transformed life through the power of God. Her story will build your confidence and faith in Jesus Christ and the power of the Holy Spirit. It is refreshing to see how God continues to work in the lives of imperfect but fully surrendered and spiritually hungry men and women. We can testify that this describes MB and we are excited to see the kingdom of God grow through her ministry.

PASTOR DAVE AND BRENDA SORENSEN

CROSSROADS ASSEMBLY OF GOD; WATERLOO, IA

Our lives are a step-by-step process of finding God's plan for our future, naturally and supernaturally. This book will take you from the old ways of defeat and darkness to God's ways of victory today and into the future. The Spirit of God is calling you forward and *Summoned out of Darkness* will show you, chapter by chapter, steps into more victory and to what the Father is calling you to be!

PASTOR RAY KELLY

DIRECTOR OF PRAYER, LIVING WORD CHRISTIAN CENTER

Powerful, inspirational and engaging... MB's book took me on a journey with her as I sat at the edge of my seat reading how God brought her from darkness to His light. Her words from the throne room entwined in the chapters of this book gave me the feeling I was next to my heavenly Father, and that He was speaking directly to me.

I already had the pleasure of being a leader with MB in Patricia King's WIMN (Women in Ministry Network) before I became her spiritual midwife to birth this amazing testimony of her life in *Summoned out of Darkness*. If you have trials you are dealing with now, or you know someone who needs encouragement in their season of life, *Summoned out of Darkness* will transport you to a heavenly realm of love, encouragement and leaning in to feel the heartbeat of King Jesus.

RHONDA F. KITABJIAN

PRESIDENT OF ROYAL BUSINESS CONSULTING

AUTHOR OF THE *JESUS AT WORK* SERIES AND *GOD ON THE MOVE*

As you read *Summoned Out of Darkness*, the shackles of your past will begin to off as you experience the love of God in a new way. MB's candid testimony will help you overcome any obstacle to accomplishing the fullness of God's plan for your life.

BRANDI BELT

OVERFLOW GLOBAL MINISTRIES

CINCINNATI, OHIO

DEDICATION TO
MY TRIUNE GOD...

Father, You have shown me Your heart.
Thank you, Abba, for revealing to me
the "Heartbeat of Heaven,"
so that I can share it with others.

To my Lord and King, Jesus Christ,
whom I am madly in love with;
Thank you for living a sinless life
and then dying for me,
so that I can live in eternity with You.

My heart bows in worship before You, Adonai.
Holy Spirit, You have guided me into all truth.
You are my comforter and my best friend.
Thank you for making me lovesick for King Jesus.

To My Precious Husband Jeff...

You are my great love, my support, and my champion.

Thank you for standing by me through the darkness.

Thank you for always believing in me.

Thank you for your faithfulness in all things.

Thank you for being a biblical husband and loving me

as Christ loves the church.

I cannot imagine my life without you.

"I delight to fulfill Your will, my God,
For Your living words are written upon the pages of my heart.
I will tell everyone everywhere the truth of Your righteousness.
And You know I haven't held back in telling the message to all.
I don't keep it a secret or hide the truth.
I preach of Your faithfulness and kindness,
proclaiming Your extravagant love to the largest crowd I can find!

Let all who passionately seek You
erupt with excitement and joy over what You've done!
Let all Your lovers rejoice continually in the Savior, saying,
"How great and glorious is our God!"

Psalm 40:8-10, 16, TPT

ACKNOWLEDGMENTS

First and foremost, I would like to thank my family.

Mom and dad… I long to reunite with you in Heaven.
Thank you for raising me the best you knew how.
Yes, times were tough… but we triumphed in the end.
Mom, I will forever be grateful to you for
praying me into the kingdom of God.

Candy, Wade and Paula…

Thank you for welcoming me back into the family.
I am so grateful for the relationship we have now;
held together by our mutual love for Jesus and each other.
All Glory to King Jesus for restoration!

To Pastors Mac and Lynne Hammond …

Pastor Mac…

Thank you for being my Gamaliel.
You are the best teacher of the Word I know.
Thank you for being faithful to never waiver,
by preaching the full counsel of God.
I am so grateful that the Lord brought me to sit
under your authority and teaching.

Pastor Lynne…

Thank you for emulating what it is to be a Proverbs 31 wife.
Your ability to flow in the Spirit has shown me what is possible
when we seek Him with all of our heart.

To my spiritual mothers Loni and Twila…

Thank you, Loni, for always being patient with me.
Thank you for never judging me when I made a mistake.
Thank you for your loving guidance.
I will see you in Heaven, sweet, sweet Loni.
Thank you, Twila, for stepping in and helping me
to become the Christian woman I am a today.
Our precious moments together are sacred to me.

To my friend Kenton…

Thank you, faithful friend, for always helping me
land on my feet during my dark days.
It has been a miracle watching you become
the man of God you are today.
Thank you for standing in for my father
and giving me away to Jeff in our wedding.
You helped save my life, and I am eternally grateful.

To my faithful intercessors…

Without your diligence to pray, and your willingness
to help birth *Summoned out of Darkness* by getting on your knees.
This book would not have been birthed.

Elizabeth, Linda, Lisa, Sandy H., Marsha, Sandy Mc., and Twila...

The glory of the Lord shines brightly upon you.

I love you all so much!

To Dr. Michelle Burkett...
Director; Women in Ministry Network (WIMN)

You have been to me, minister, counselor, administrator
and most of all, friend.

Thank you for taking a chance on me,
to help you steward the precious women in our network.

To my spiritual daughters...

You have been a most precious gift to me from the Lord.
Iron sharpens iron. You all sharpen me beyond measure.
I am truly grateful for each one of you.

Finally, to my spiritual midwife Rhonda Kitabjian.
President; Royal Business Consulting
Rhonda, you amaze me.

Summoned out of Darkness was birthed because of you.
Your faithfulness to help me push and deliver this baby
was so supernatural and so incredibly beautiful.

God brought us together in forever friendship and sisterhood.
All I can say is wow. What a God-sent gift you are.

TABLE OF CONTENTS

FOREWORD

MB Busch's book, *Summoned Out of Darkness,* is not merely a warm testimonial of God's healing love and His grace to sinners, but in many ways, it is a spiritual road map displaying the pathway of God's redemptive power for all believers today, regardless of their own set of personal traumas, difficulties, and weaknesses. The Lord Jesus taught His disciples to pray, "on earth as it is in heaven" (Matthew 6:10) and you will feel the heart-beat of heaven in every page of this story of the author's grace-filled pilgrimage into His glory. Glory! As the apostle Paul said, "Do everything for the glory of God" (1 Corinthians 10:31). We all begin in the Father and we all will end up back at the throne of God facing the Father, for all things come from Him and all things return to Him (Acts 17:28; Romans 11:36). Therefore, we should all earnestly desire to enter into and experience His glory on earth now! Now faith is a present-day experience, not a future one (Hebrews 1:1).

Jesus Christ, the Lord of Glory (1 Corinthians 2:8), is also in charge of the process that brings us out of sin and shame and into fullness and glory. It was always the ultimate intention of God that you walk every day in His glory, just as Adam did in the Garden of Eden (Genesis 3). He never stops moving us upward to greater things, higher levels of revelation and power.

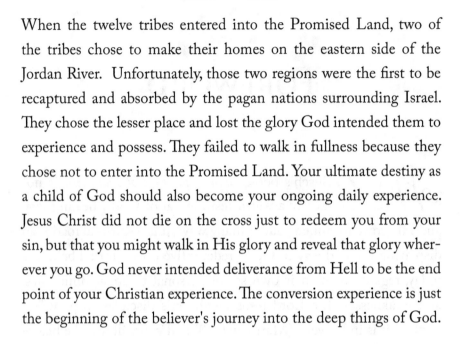

When the twelve tribes entered into the Promised Land, two of the tribes chose to make their homes on the eastern side of the Jordan River. Unfortunately, those two regions were the first to be recaptured and absorbed by the pagan nations surrounding Israel. They chose the lesser place and lost the glory God intended them to experience and possess. They failed to walk in fullness because they chose not to enter into the Promised Land. Your ultimate destiny as a child of God should also become your ongoing daily experience. Jesus Christ did not die on the cross just to redeem you from your sin, but that you might walk in His glory and reveal that glory wherever you go. God never intended deliverance from Hell to be the end point of your Christian experience. The conversion experience is just the beginning of the believer's journey into the deep things of God.

Thankfully, in these last days, God is once again raising up a holy remnant to steward His revelation and release His glory on the earth. MB Busch's story is really the story of everyone because the revelation she has received and the glory (2 Corinthians 12:2) that she has experienced is truly the birthright of every born-again believer. She is one of a new company of heaven-sent agents God has chosen as a witness (1 Corinthians. 4:1) of God's great love and to motivate others to reach for a more wonderful life now.

In her book, she shares the process God used to first redeem her and then to guide her into real fullness. Like the two tribes who failed to enter into the Promised Land and made their homes on the east side of the Jordan river, too many Christians lose touch with the purposes of God in their lives and settle for the things of this world while forfeiting the glory of God. I don't want you to miss out on anything Jesus died to give you. It is my prayer that you take the teachings in this book seriously, enter fully into all the promises of God, and walk in His glory.

Summoned Out of Darkness is the kind of work that speaks powerfully to this generation, because this generation has largely left the biblical revelation behind as it has sought for joy and meaning apart from God. MB Busch's testimony and what she learned is perfectly written to speak to them (2 Corinthians 1:4). I believe that the life of heaven and the power of God as portrayed in this book will help you experience what was always meant for every child of God – for *you*, Beloved. I suggest you digest the contents of this book and trust God to do a similar work in your life.

Blessings,

JOAN HUNTER
JOAN HUNTER MINISTRIES

Introduction

The Lord God has given me the tongue of the learned,
That I should know how to speak a word in season
to him who is weary.
He awakens me morning by morning…
He awakens My ear, to hear as the learned.

– Isaiah 50:4, NKJV –

Friends invite… but kings summon.

*A*nd that is precisely what happened to me in October 2007. I was "summoned out of darkness" by King Jesus. Prior to that, I was cold and lifeless to the things of God.

I was raised in an alcoholic home where dysfunction flourished. I was drenched in fear for most of my childhood, as emotional abuse and rejection occurred on a regular basis. Because I did not know the love of a Savior, I felt hopeless and defeated. Nowhere to run and nowhere to hide… I was utterly tormented by the darkness that surrounded me. Fear morphed into self-destruction, and I became a train wreck speeding towards death.

There used to be an old Corningware television commercial jingle that went, "From the freezer… to the oven…to the table." That jingle is the theme that frames my testimony. From a frozen heart to the fiery furnace, to the Lord's table, is where you'll find yourself as you journey with me through the pages of this book.

I know everyone has had struggles in life, and some of you may be going through some right now, but there's incredible hope! The biblical story of Joseph tells of how he went from the pit to the palace. That is exactly what happened to me. God lifted me out of the pit I had fallen into and set me high upon a Rock – Jesus – and He will do the same for you.

Beloved, your circumstances are not a surprise to God. He is with you in the storms of life, and if you allow Him to be the Captain of your ship, you will sail smoothly through them.

Trust in the Lord with all your heart, and lean not on your own understanding; In all your ways acknowledge Him, and He shall direct your paths. —Proverbs 3:5-6, NKJV

Allow Holy Spirit to speak to you as you read through the pages of this book. He told me that He would drizzle honey on each page. Did you know that honey in the Bible was an honored gift?

Then their father Israel said; "If it must be, then do this: Put some of the "best products" of the land in your bags and take them down to the man as a gift - a little balm and a little honey, some spices and myrrh, some pistachio nuts and almonds."

—Genesis 43:11, ESV

In other words, this book is an "honored gift" to you from Holy Spirit. I am merely the vessel He will work though, to bring you encouragement, love, and hope. No matter where you are in life, He will speak to your individual circumstances.

The last part of the book is titled "The Heartbeat of Heaven; Love Declarations from the Father's Heart." This section contains words directly from the secret place of the Father's heart to yours. These "Throne Room" words will address your destiny and the Father's love towards you. As I type these words, He is showing me beautiful gemstones falling from Heaven on you, the reader.

My story is both inspiring, and at times, terrifying. It is my prayer that you will find yourself in these pages. I welcome you into this journey. Along the way, I not only use scripture but song lyrics as well. Holy Spirit is supernaturally giving me music as I write, lyrics that are applicable to the text. May the Lord speak to your heart on every page, beloved.

He sent from above, He took me;
He drew me out of many waters.
He delivered me from my strong enemy,
from those who hated me,
for they were too strong for me.
They confronted me in the day of my calamity,
but the Lord was my support.
He also brought me out into a broad place;
He delivered me because He delighted in me.

– Psalm 18:16-19, NKJV

PART ONE
From the Freezer...

You're as cold as ice

You're willing to sacrifice our love

You never take advice

Someday you'll pay the price, I know

"Cold as Ice"_ (As sung by Foreigner)
Lyrics: Lou Gramm / Mick Jones

Chapter One

MY TRAIN WRECK LIFE

Oh, mama mia, mama mia, mama mia, let me go
Beelzebub has a devil put aside for me
For me, for me, for me.[1]

LIFE IN THE CARNIVAL

Have you ever ridden the tilt-a-whirl? You know… that ride that spins and jerks you around?

My life growing up was forever spinning out of control. My emotions were jerked continuously back and forth and up and down. The only thing that was constant was that nothing ever stayed the same.

There was such an age difference between my siblings and me, that I was basically raised as an only child. My sister Candy got married and had moved to California when I was ten, and my brother Wade had moved into the fraternity house at the local university when I was eleven. During my formative years, my mother was an alcoholic, and my father suffered from manic depression – generally recognized today as bipolar disorder. The highs were high, and the

---

1 "Bohemian Rhapsody"; lyrics by Freddie Mercury. (As sung by Queen)

lows were devastatingly low. The emotional and verbal abuse in my home was frightening to me as a child.

Growing up, I did not have control over my circumstances. Obviously, I could not leave home, so I left home in my mind. This ultimately led me to create a new me – the perfect me. My made-up life was void of any problems. So those who "saw" me, it was as if they had taken a trip to the fun house. In a fun house, all the mirrors show a distorted image of what a person "looks like." People saw what I wanted them to see… a false image of myself.

Welcome to my double life. To the onlooker, my life looked utterly envious on the outside. By the time I was in junior high and high school, I had orchestrated my dream persona. I was the ultimate overachiever; excellent grades, on the cheerleading squad, in drama, student council, glee club, and band. I was the popular one who always had a boyfriend and too many girlfriends to count. I became the consummate play-actor of my own life.

If they had only known the ugly truth. My virginity was stolen from me by a boyfriend who date-raped me when I was a sophomore in high school. My girlfriends' parents were out of town, so she had a party. We were all drinking, of course, and he raped me underneath the pool table. I was so traumatized by this event, that for years, I blocked this trauma out of my mind and believed that I had lost my virginity to my college boyfriend. But even though I was not consciously aware of it, subconsciously, the rape made me feel dirty and ugly on the inside. It also fueled the intense desire to make myself look perfect to the outside world.

I kept as many plates spinning in the air as I could to keep me busy after school. I hated walking through the front door at home. I

felt such shame. I dared not even have a girlfriend spend the night, because then they would find out who the "real me" was. Everyone clamored to be my friend, yet I wanted to die inside.

About the time I was fifteen years old, my father put my mom in treatment. She got sober and found Jesus; all in the same year. I should have been ecstatic, but I didn't understand this "Jesus thing." I thought God was mad at me and ashamed of me. I had been fed so many lies by the denominational church I was raised in. I was never taught about the love of a Savior, or that Jesus shed His blood so that I could be forgiven of all my sins. After my mom met Jesus, she dragged to me to hear various evangelists that came to town. I even said the salvation prayer. I didn't mean it, though, because I was so filled with self-loathing. I did not believe in my heart that He actually died for "me."

WRONG BELIEFS I WAS TAUGHT

I was taught by the denomination that I was raised in, that If I was *good enough*, I might get to go to Heaven. I was not taught the Bible and I believed the only way I could connect with God, confess my sins and ask for forgiveness was through a church priest. If you are unaware of this, the Levitical priesthood was abolished after the cross. Jesus is our High-Priest now, and He alone. The veil was torn when He cried out, "It is finished!" We now have complete access to the Throne of Grace without having to go through a priest. God desires a personal relationship with YOU. Jesus died ONE TIME for all of your sins… past, present, and future. You do not need to go through a priest for forgiveness of sins; and prayer is beautiful conversation you have with the Lord – not penance.

Another wrong belief my denomination taught is that infant baptism gets you into Heaven –nowhere in the Bible does it say this. I could elaborate on that one point for an entire chapter, but I won't. Just know that the Word of God trumps any man-made tradition. If infant baptism got you into Heaven, then why did Jesus say you must be born again? The decision to accept Christ as your personal Savior is one that can only be made by you, and not anyone standing in your place.

Beloved, you can't earn the free gift of salvation. Jesus lived the perfect life for you, so that He could qualify to be your living sacrifice. He shed the blood required, to atone for your sin and die in your place.

> If you confess with your mouth the Lord Jesus, and believe in your heart that God has raised Him from the dead, you will be saved. – Romans 10:9, NKJV

If you do not know Jesus yet, call on Him now. Repent of your sins and ask Him to come into your heart and be your Lord and Savior. If you have just done that for the first time, you have received the miracle gift of salvation!

Also, did you know that you can continue to take Holy Communion if you are divorced?

> And He took bread, gave thanks and broke it, and gave it to them, saying, "This is My body which is given for you; do this in remembrance of Me." Likewise, He also took the cup after supper, saying, "This cup is the new covenant in My blood, which is shed for you." – Luke 22:19-20, NKJV

Jesus said, "Do this in remembrance of Me." He did not say; "Do this *only* if the host is blessed by a priest, and you are not divorced. Friend, if you have been taught to believe that, then I would encourage you to stop what you are doing right now and take Holy Communion in your home. It is a symbolic act of the Blood Covenant that Jesus died to give you. You can use grape juice and bread or crackers at home. As you take communion in your home, thank Him for the sacrifice that was accomplished for you on Calvary. My husband Jeff and I do it every morning to celebrate our blood covenant with the Lord and to stand on everything that Jesus shed blood to give us.

LET THE GAMES BEGIN

Now, back to my self-destructive life. I began my death journey in high school. The drinking age law changed to 18 when I was a senior in high school. I turned 18 in January of my senior year, so even though I had already been drinking for several years, alcohol was now freely accessible. As I look back, I can clearly see the downward spiral that my life was taking. Drinking was woven into the fabric of my life. It started out as social partying, but I was hooked, and it medicated all the pain I was experiencing.

Sex, drugs, and rock and roll were the theme of my life as I began college. Even though I prided myself that I was never a one-night-stand kind of gal, I always had two or three boyfriends at the same time, and I slept with all of them. In other words, I was sexually promiscuous. I felt so dirty and worthless on the inside, but the alcohol did a great job at medicating my pain.

I also became bulimic in college. One of the girls from a sorority that was "rushing" me shared with me that I could eat anything I wanted and not gain weight. All I had to do was throw up my food after I ate. This sounded too good to be true. Little did I know that it was the beginning of a 30-year, three times a day compulsion that could have killed me at any moment.

They tell you that bulimia is a coping mechanism that people use to control something in their chaotic lives, but the truth is, it is demonic oppression of the severest kind.

I was introduced to cocaine in college as well, and it was love at first snort. It allowed me to drink all I wanted to and not get drunk. My deception had now hit the catastrophic level, and I was living a trifecta of self-destruction – drugs, alcohol, and bulimia. In less than two years, I went from being on the University's Dean's List with a 3.5 grade average to academic probation. Nothing seemed to matter other than how I felt. I was numbing my pain with alcohol and drugs, binging and purging food, and having sex with multiple partners. As this chapter is appropriately titled, it was my "My Train Wreck Life."

If you are in pain right now and are running from God, know this: No matter how far you have fallen…. God's arm is not too short to pull you out! His great love and mercy are unfathomable. There is no sin too great that the shed blood of Jesus did not cover. Cry out to Him, and He will pull you out! He loves YOU beyond measure!

Listen! The LORD's arm is not too weak to save you, nor is his ear too deaf to hear you call. – Isaiah 59:1, NLT

Sewn Together by the Father's Love

My precious child…

There is no variation or turning inside of Me.
The fragments of your life are pieces of My heart
sewn together by My great love for you.
You have been bought with a price, My royal one.
Soak in My mercy and love towards you.

Jehovah Shammah

Every good gift and every perfect gift is from above,
and comes down from the Father of lights,
with whom there is no variation or
shadow of turning. *— James 1:17*

My downward death-spiral continued and I rode the spin cycle of a merry-go-round. I married my first husband when I was 23 – he ended up being someone with an insatiable need to control me. When I look back, I think I looked to him to save me, but it was a disaster. Neither one of us knew Jesus. We were clueless that marriage was a covenant with God, not merely a legal contract. The Bible says;

A threefold cord is not quickly broken. – Ecclesiastes 4:12, NKJV

In other words, with Jesus interwoven into the fabric of your marriage, it is not easily breakable. But this was not the case with my first marriage, and it broke up after three years.

31

My destructive patterns continued into my 30s and 40s. The self-abuse continued to be the same, I just became older, and the merry-go-round was far from merry. A geographical relocation didn't work either. In my early 40s, I moved to North Carolina for another relationship that ultimately did not work out. I left a wide swath of destruction there too. I hurt many people, but I was too numb to care. I was void of any feeling, and the devil had me in his evil clutches.

During that time, my dad passed away. He left me a six-figure inheritance that I blew on me, myself and I. I was so soaked in self-centeredness! It got so bad in North Carolina that I had to escape. My family had written me off back home, and I had burned all the bridges I had faultily constructed in my life.

I returned home to Minnesota in 2005, but the craziness continued. I felt hopeless and ashamed. I joined the community of Alcoholics Anonymous upon my return, thinking that through osmosis, that would save me. If only I had known the truth; that addiction was demonic oppression, and that the ONLY thing that could set me free was the blood of Jesus.

In September 2006 I was driving in downtown Minneapolis in an alcoholic blackout and took out a bike rack upon driving onto the curb of a famous nightclub. The police hauled me off to jail, and it was there that I came to the end of myself. I realized that if there had been an event there that night, I could have killed someone. The next morning after I was released from jail, I reached out to my friend Kenton.

He was the only friend I had left in the world after moving back home to Minneapolis from North Carolina. We had met 30 years

before, and he had watched me plunge deeper into despair. He felt helpless and did not know where to turn to get me help, so he called my sister Candy. He told her that if I did not get the help I needed, I would die. She and her husband Al were moved by compassion and offered to pay financially for my treatment. In October 2006, I entered a treatment facility in Wayzata, Minnesota. Thank you, Holy Spirit, for guiding them to take the action that would ultimately lead to my sobriety.

ON THE ROAD TO RECOVERY

When I entered the treatment center that October, I knew I had come to the end of the road in my addiction. It was either sober up or die. I had faked my way through other treatments in the past, because at the time, I was not ready to get sober. I most certainly was ready now, though, to get free of this bondage. Little did I know that God, Creator of the Universe, had started working on my heart. I did not know this God yet ... but I was about to see His providence in my life.

On the third day of treatment, I saw this stunning man sitting on the sofa in the foyer. When he said hello, my heart melted. For the duration of our time there, we seemed to always end up next to each other in meetings and in the dining hall. He said he had lost his first wife Pam to alcoholism and that he was serious about getting sober. Little did I know that God had orchestrated our steps to meet. That man turned out to be my future husband, Jeff. We were two broken people that the Lord brought together. He knew that we would eventually radically fall in love with His son Jesus and each other and go on to serve Him. Beloved, can you think of a time where God intervened on your behalf? The Bible says that He loved us while we were first sinners.

> But Christ proved God's passionate love for us by dying in our place while we were still lost and ungodly! – Romans 5:8, TPT

It was unfathomable to me that God loved me, let alone that He died for me. But the truth remained, and God was proving it to me. Cherished one, God knows the end from the beginning; He saw me in the deepest darkness and yet He still loved me enough to pull me out of my despair. He will do the same for you too!

THE GLIMMER OF A BETTER LIFE

Once Jeff and I completed our treatment and left the center, we immediately started dating. Many of our nights out consisted of going to AA meetings three-four times a week, and we ended up making the meetings themselves our higher power. At the meetings we were taught that alcoholism is an incurable disease, and that the only way to maintain sobriety was to work the 12 steps. No one told us the biblical truth; that Jesus took ALL sickness and disease when He was scourged and that we could be healed and walk free of it!

> But He was wounded for our transgressions, He was bruised for our iniquities; The chastisement for our peace was upon Him, and by His stripes we are healed. – Isaiah 53:5, NKJV

At these meetings, we were also continually confessing that our identity was found in our addiction. We did not know at that time

that our identity would be in Christ and that the power of life and death were in the tongue.

> Death and life are in the power of the tongue, and those who love it and indulge it will eat its fruit and bear the consequences of their words. – Proverbs 18:21, AMP

They say that only 17% of people that go through traditional treatment stay sober. Precious one, there is a 100% rate of success in Jesus Christ and Him alone. Every time I introduced myself in these meetings by saying; "Hi, my name is MB, and I AM an alcoholic," I was prophesying that into being. Don't get me wrong, the fellowship of AA and other 12-step programs are wonderful and I am not throwing the baby out with the bathwater. The point I am making is that alcoholism is NOT an incurable disease. I implore you not to confess your identity in addiction if you are struggling right now. Cry out to Jesus, and He will come running!

Jeff and I continued to walk in sobriety, but something was missing. We thought, *We are in a "spiritual" program of recovery, so how can something be missing?* We were about to find out.

Chapter Two

THE POSTER CHILD FOR REDEMPTION

If you change your mind, I'm the first in line,
Honey, I'm still free, take a chance on Me.
If you need Me, let me know, I'm going to be around.
If you've got no place to go, if you're feeling down.
If you're all alone when the pretty birds have flown,
Honey, I'm still free, take a chance on Me. [2]

THIS THE WAY...WALK IN IT

Take a Chance on Me by "Abba" is playing in my head as I write this. Remember in my introduction, I told you that Holy Spirit gives me music? Abba is the Hebrew word meaning, "Daddy." Holy Spirit has been playing that song in my heart since I started writing this book.

---

2 "Take a Chance on Me"; Lyrics by Benny Goran Bror Andersson / Bjoern K Ulvaeus. (As Sung by Abba)

In fact, He asked me to put the lyrics in this book for you, the reader. Is He wooing you, right now? Maybe He is calling you to Him for the first time.

Maybe you have stepped away, and He is calling you home. No matter where you are in your life, the door is always open. This is what your Savior is saying to you right now: *Come drink from the Well of Salvation (Isaiah 12:3).*

FOUND: THE MISSING LINK

Jeff and I had been sober now for exactly one year, yet we knew that there was more to spirituality than the higher power we heard about in Alcoholics Anonymous. One Friday afternoon, I was talking with my new friend Julie Ann, who asked me what I was doing over the weekend. I told her that Jeff and I were looking for a church to attend. She suggested that Jeff and I meet her and her husband Bobby at their church on Sunday morning – (a "Word of Faith" church).

I immediately said yes, and the rest is history! When we walked into the church and heard the true gospel preached for the first time; we knew that we knew, that we had found our new home. When I heard the Word of God preached for the first time, it was like a pinball machine to me; ding, ding, ding, ding! Jeff said he felt like Elizabeth, as John the Baptist leaped in her womb when Mary, who was pregnant with Jesus, came to visit.

It was not until the second time we attended, that they gave an altar call. We raced to the altar and gave our lives to Jesus. Getting born again changed everything. We had discovered the *missing link,* and it was Jesus! This church, where we gave our lives to Jesus, is where we now serve.

DIVING HEAD FIRST INTO THE JESUS POOL

Jesus said, "You will know the truth, and the truth will set you free." What Jesus was referring to was His good news, the Gospel. We realized that we had been starving to death our entire lives for the Truth. No wonder they call Jesus, the "Bread of Life." I am not exaggerating when I say that Jeff and I were raised from the dead. We had found life itself, and Jesus died for us to have it. He wants you to have it too. He is calling you now.

Leap of Faith

My child…

A precious prize and portion will be bestowed unto you…

because of your willingness.

My manifest glory will be present upon you,

as you run breathlessly into the wind of My Spirit!

Take a calculated risk and jump off a cliff into new frontiers.

Take a leap of faith and dive headfirst

into a pool of righteousness and truth!

This is My glory! This is My kingdom!

Reparations will be made to you, My precious one.

Righteousness, peace and holiness shall follow you

all the days of your life,

and you shall dwell with me in My house forever.

~Christ the Lord~

I now know what Mary felt like after she had a visit from the angel Gabriel. I felt unspeakable joy for the very first time in my life. After becoming born again, there were times I would have to pull over when driving because I would be weeping with gratitude. There are still times now that I am so overcome with gratitude that I weep. Waves of mercy and grace wash over me as God pours out His love upon me.

> I'm bursting with God-news; I'm dancing the song of my Savior God. God took one good look at me, and look what happened— I'm the most fortunate woman on earth! What God has done for me will never be forgotten, the God whose very name is holy, set apart from all others. His mercy flows in wave after wave on those who are in awe before him.
>
> – Luke 1:46-49, MSG

If you have never felt that love before, He is waiting to pour out His love on you. Stop reading right now and ask Him to shower you with His endless love. Friend, it does not matter how much you have sinned. Jesus shed blood for every sin you have ever committed or will commit in the future. He loves you! He died for YOU!

When I've look back on my life and where I had been, I've realized that I was the notorious sinful woman in Luke 7:36-50 where Jesus says, "Those that have been forgiven much, love much."

> Then one of the Pharisees asked Him to eat with him. And He went to the Pharisee's house and sat down to eat. And behold, a woman in the city who was a sinner, when she knew that Jesus sat at the table in the Pharisee's house, brought an alabaster flask of fragrant oil, and stood at His feet behind Him

weeping; and she began to wash His feet with her tears and wiped them with the hair of her head; and she kissed His feet and anointed them with the fragrant oil.

The Feet of Jesus

Beautiful Child…

Kiss the feet of your Savior

and worship Me at the Mercy Seat,

as I pour out My Spiritual rain upon you,

called forth by Me, your living God;

to accomplish kingdom purposes that I have set forth.

In the day of trouble I will confine you

in the protection of My armor.

Walk stealthily through the Vineyard.

Exousia authority will carry you through the trials of life.[3]

Your King ravishes you with His love.

Now when the Pharisee who had invited Him saw this, he spoke to himself, saying, "This Man, if He were a prophet, would know who and what manner of woman this is who is touching Him, for she is a sinner."

And Jesus answered and said to him, "Simon, I have something to say to you." So, he said, "Teacher, say it."

---

3 Exousia is the original Greek word usually translated as authority or power. The name of Jesus carries all authority in Heaven and Earth.

"There was a certain creditor who had two debtors. One owed five hundred denarii, and the other fifty. And when they had nothing with which to repay, he freely forgave them both. Tell Me, therefore, which of them will love him more?" Simon answered and said, "I suppose the one whom he forgave more."

And He said to him, "You have rightly judged." Then He turned to the woman and said to Simon, "Do you see this woman? I entered your house; you gave Me no water for My feet, but she has washed My feet with her tears and wiped them with the hair of her head.

"You gave Me no kiss, but this woman has not ceased to kiss My feet since the time I came in. You did not anoint My head with oil, but this woman has anointed My feet with fragrant oil.

"Therefore I say to you, her sins, which are many, are forgiven, for she loved much. But to whom little is forgiven, the same loves little." – Luke 7:36-50, NKJV

CLEAN-UP

I also soon discovered that Holy Spirit doesn't do His clean-up job on new believers overnight. God not only is merciful, but all so ever patient. The very first thing He dealt with me about was my mouth and my attire. I was not a big swearer, but I did say, "Oh, my God" constantly. Shortly after I was saved, I said it, and it came out "Oh, my gosh." I said "God," but it came out "gosh." Wow! Also, all my dresses became tops. Have you ever felt the nudging of Holy Spirit on you to make a change? He convicts – not condemns. The Bible says, 'There is no condemnation in those that are in Christ Jesus" (Romans 8:1).

Jeff and I were living together in fornication when we were saved. We did not know that sex outside of marriage was a sin. No one had told us that sex was created by God and was a gift to a husband and a wife for procreation and pleasure. Sex between a husband and a wife is holy and is a blessing to the covenant of marriage.

After being saved for about three months, every time we had sex, all I could think about was Jesus. I felt awful. I called Loni, a woman I had met at church, and asked her if sex outside of marriage was a sin, and she was delighted to answer me. (Loni eventually became my spiritual mom.)

She said, "Yes, honey it is." I then told Jeff about it, but his flesh did not want to receive that. I continued to have sex with him under great fear of losing him, so I called Loni to pray with me that Jeff would be convicted. God answered our prayer!

The very next Sunday, Pastor Mac was preaching that "willful" (intentional) sin blocked the blessings of God. Led by Holy Spirit, he walked over to where Jeff was sitting and looked right at Jeff and said these words: "Sex outside of marriage is a sin." Yay, God! As we were walking out of church, Jeff looked at me and said, "I need the blessings of God more than I need sex." We then went to our associate pastor and took a vow of celibacy until we were to get married, four months later. Beloved, if you are being convicted of anything right now, cry out to Jesus and repent. He has already shed blood for your sin and is waiting for you to ask for forgiveness.

At this juncture in my writing, I cannot impress upon you enough the importance of knowing the Word. Remember that Jesus said, "You will know the truth (the Word), and the truth will set you free." It will set you free from the lies of the enemy because they most definitely will come. Did you know that before bankers had special pens to detect counterfeit money, they did not study counterfeit bills, only the real ones? That way, when the counterfeit was presented; they could distinguish the real from the fake.

That is the way it is with the Bible. If you know the truth of the Word, then when the devil comes to kill, steal and destroy, you can come back at him with the truth of who you really are. Jesus did that in the wilderness when the devil came to tempt Him. He said, "It is written" and then quoted scriptural truth back at the devil. (See Matthew and Luke chapter 4.) It also says;

Resist the Devil and he WILL flee from you. – James 4:7, NKJV

I encourage you to start reading a chapter in Proverbs, a Psalm and a few chapters in the gospel each day. It will only require a few minutes. Jesus hung on the cross for you, beloved, for six hours. Can you get up a few minutes earlier and start your day with Jesus? It will change your life, I promise! Once you get in a regular pattern of reading the Word, you will want more! It is a supernatural phenomenon. It is like taking your spirit man to the gym. It gets stronger and stronger the more you do it.

So then faith comes by hearing, and hearing by the Word of God. – Romans 10:17, NKJV

I used to play "Bible Bingo," but I do not encourage it. I would flip open my Bible, and wherever it would land, I would read. Be intentional about what to read, and God will bless it.

HE WHO THE SON SETS FREE
IS FREE INDEED

Exactly 90 days after getting born again, we were baptized in the Holy Spirit. As soon as Pastor Mac laid hands on us, we were both "slain in the Spirit" and went down on the floor under the power of God. We both literally felt something lift off of us. We came up completely set free. The desire to use drugs, drink alcohol or binge and purge food was completely taken from me. The oppression was totally gone. We had just received a creative miracle!

Also, after I was baptized in the Holy Spirit, my life went from black and white to technicolor. Everything was intensified in the Word of God and I began to go deeper and deeper in the scriptures. I could not get enough. I was insatiable for the Word of God. I actually was excited when going to bed at night, because I could wake up in the morning and read the Word.

I was on a journey with Jesus, and I was madly in love. One morning, I was missing my mom. She had died in 1996, and I was high on cocaine when she died. What a disaster. I was so un-spiritually fit to lose her. When I was on my knees one morning after praise and worship; I asked the Lord, "Does my mom know I love you?" He answered, "Daughter... she prayed you in!"

The effective, fervent prayer of a righteous man (woman) avails much. – James 5:16, NKJV

Wow! A drug-addicted, alcoholic, bulimic, adulteress, lying thief had been prayed into the Kingdom of God. How spectacular is that? If you have a lost loved one that does not know Jesus, stop reading and pray for them right now. Jesus is waiting to answer your prayer petition.

Chapter 3

THE JEREMIAH CALLING

Then the word of the Lord came to me, saying:
"Before I formed you in the womb I knew you;
Before you were born I sanctified you;
I ordained you a prophet to the nations."

– *Jeremiah 1:5, NKJV* –

CALLED FORTH FROM THE WOMB

Several months after becoming Spirit-filled in 2008; I was lying in bed before getting up one morning. I felt the holy presence of the Lord come into the room, and He spoke Jeremiah 1:5 to me. I thought to myself, *WHAT? Doesn't He know who I am? Why ME? I don't even know what this means. How can this be?* I felt like Mary, the mother of Jesus after she was told that she would give birth to the Messiah. She asked the angel Gabriel, "How can this be, since I have not been intimate with a man?" But there was a difference... I DID know a man intimately, and His name was

Jesus. Jesus was calling me forth from the womb to be His prophet to the nations.

Immediately, from that point on, I started experiencing prophetic dreams and visions at an accelerated rate. Whenever He spoke to me, I would journal everything He said. I heard His voice as I went about my day; and there are no English words to accurately describe what was happening to me. It was as though God plucked me out of my life and placed me into a new one. I lived and breathed in the supernatural realm.

One thing that was absolutely crucial, however, was that I remained grounded in the Word. Everything He showed me and spoke to me, I verified in the Word. Thank you, Pastor Mac, for admonishing us to always confirm everything in the Word.

DID GOD REALLY SAY THAT?

The serpent was the shrewdest of all the wild animals the Lord God had made. One day he asked the woman, "Did God really say you must not eat the fruit from any of the trees in the garden?" – Genesis 3:1, NKJV

The enemy loves to bring confusion, and he attempts to steal the prophetic word from us. He would often say to me; "Did God really say that?" Because everything that God said to me was backed up in the Word, I could say, "YES! God really said that!"

The last section of this book , "The Heartbeat of Heaven; Love Declarations from the Father's Heart" contains beautiful prophecies from the Throne Room that were spoken for you. Each of these words is supported by scripture. Oh, how He loves you, beloved!

I could not get enough Word. I was insatiable! I started getting up at 4:00 AM just to worship Jesus, pray to the Father and read the Word. I absolutely could not get enough of Jesus. He started speaking to me in so different many ways! In the following section I share some of these – they are not in sequential order, as I am sharing them in relation to different aspects of this story.

Then [with a deep longing] you will seek Me and require Me [as a vital necessity] and [you will] find Me when you search for Me with all your heart. – Jeremiah 29:13, AMP

CLOSE ENCOUNTERS OF THE GOD KIND

One night when I was lying in bed trying to fall asleep, I had a vision of a fetus in a bubble that was peacefully floating around the bedroom. All I knew was that it was my spiritual baby, and it meant I was going to birth something. (More on that later).

Another time, at the beginning of my calling; I had a vision of what I thought was a science experiment. I saw a cauldron that contained an amber liquid. It suddenly started bubbling up and eventually formed a fountain. I later learned that this was how a "Nabi" Prophet received things. *Nabi* is the Hebrew word for the "official" prophet. In Hebrew, *Nabi* is from a root meaning "to bubble forth, as from a fountain," hence "to utter."[4]

I later found out that the color amber in a dream or vision represents the glory of God. All Glory to King Jesus! Holy Spirit was showing me by that vision, that all of His words contain His Glory. Amen to that!

4 (Biblestudytools.com)

On Sunday, May 1st, 2011, I was startled out of bed. It was as though an army marching band was in my bedroom. I woke up to the song "Stars and Stripes." I flew out of bed, with my heart racing. I looked over at Jeff, who he was sound asleep. I then heard the words; "rabble-rouser." This means "agitator, troublemaker, instigator, firebrand, revolutionary, and insurgent." I had no idea why the Lord said this, but I would soon find out.

Later that day, after we returned home from church, Jeff went out to mow the lawn. I was reading the Word on the sofa in our family room and all of a sudden, I heard these words loudly and audibly, "WE GOT HIM!" I was so startled that I jumped off the sofa. I thought, *What? Is this connected to rabble-rouser? I know I'm not to lean on my own understanding* (Proverbs 3:5). But this was too weird not to think about.

The next morning, I woke up to the headline in the paper; "WE GOT HIM!" These were the exact words that President Obama yelled when our Marines killed Osama Bin Laden, in the early morning hours of May 2nd, 2011. When I heard those words on my sofa, God was revealing to me the future, because his assassination had not happened yet. This was a teachable moment for me. God was showing me that His Word is true and used this encounter as an example of the following scripture:

Surely the Lord God does nothing, unless He reveals His secret to His servants the prophets. – Amos 3:7, NKJV

Beloved, God knows the end from the beginning, for He is omniscient, (all knowing). It says in the Word:

For **I know** the plans and thoughts that I have for you,' says the Lord, 'plans for peace and well-being and not for disaster, to give you a future and a hope. – Jeremiah 29:11, AMP

God has already written each day of your life in your "Book of Life" in Heaven, as He knows the end from the beginning. He WILL lead you down the path of your destiny, if you look to Him and get to know Him through His Word. Now would be a good time to stop reading this book and read Psalm 139, to see how the Father feels towards you. It is an amazing Psalm, and I hope it will minister to you, as it has so many times to me. As David writes, it is unmeasurable – the amount He loves us.

In addition to the above, I had several other unique encounters I feel led to share with you. One night when I was lying in bed talking to Jeff, I had a headline scroll across the ceiling in my bedroom. It was like one of those advertising banners you see pulled behind small planes. God is so cool!

Also, two weeks before we went to Israel in 2010, I was sitting on the sofa in the family room when I heard the audible voice of God. He said; "Five bushels of wheat are now four." He took seven years to give me the revelation, bit by bit. I could write a book on that word alone, but it would be a rabbit trail which I choose not to go down in this writing. I've shared these examples with you to show you that the Lord speaks to us in various ways. He will guide you and train you in the ways that are tailored specifically to your calling. Isn't that amazing? You are called to fulfill your destiny!

ENTERING THE COURT OF MAN

Do you remember that I shared with you that I received a creative miracle after I became spirit-filled in January 2008? In an instant, all demonic oppression left me and my body was supernaturally healed from the ravages of bondage to drugs, alcohol and bulimia. Eight weeks later, I had a life-changing trip to the mailbox. I opened up the mailbox and pulled out a big packet. It was from the criminal division of the county I lived in. I opened it and discovered that they had charged me with eight felonies for bad checks I had written, going back as far as nine years. I had done that during the train wreck part of my life. That all stopped when I got sober in 2006, one year before I met Jesus.

Four thoughts entered my mind: 1.) *This is a piece of cake for Jesus!* I had just received my creative miracle, and what He did for me once, He would do again. 2.) *I am the daughter that He loves.* 3.) *I'm His prophet-in training, therefore; He will never allow me to go to prison.* 4.) *You can't prosecute a "dead man."*

> I have been crucified with Christ; it is no longer I who live, but Christ lives in me. – Galatians 2:20, NKJV

So… what's a Word-of-Faith girl going to do? She is going to speak to her mountain, of course. This court process dragged out over the next three years, and every day I confessed the same thing;

> "In Jesus name, and upon the authority of His holy word; I speak to my mountain which is this court case; may you be lifted up into the sea and be disposed of. I believe it in my heart and do not doubt in my mind, that it will come to pass."
> – Mark 11:23-24, NKJV

All this time, I had thought that my life in the carnival had ended, but I was in for the ride of my life, called the "emotional rollercoaster." I was determined that the devil would not prevail.

Have you ever been blindsided by the enemy? This is what the Lord says to you today:

Jeweled

The issues of life are not what you make them

when you relegate responsibility to your Messiah.

The answers come swiftly and beautifully.

You are indescribably beautiful, My child.

Recompense awaits you.

Fear not, My little one....

My manifest presence encases you in glory.

You are jeweled. You are My treasure!

~Christ the King~

I also love The Message Translation's version of the following scripture.

Be prepared. You're up against far more than you can handle on your own. Take all the help you can get, every weapon God has issued, so that when it's all over but the shouting you'll still be on your feet. Truth, righteousness, peace, faith, and salvation are more than words. Learn how to apply them. You'll need them throughout your life. God's Word is an indispensable weapon. – Ephesians 6:13-17, MSG

Chapter 4

YOU CAN'T PROSECUTE A DEAD MAN

Well you're a real tough cookie (Devil) with a long history

Of breaking little hearts like the one in me

That's okay, let's see how you do it,

put up your dukes, let's get down to it

Hit me with your best shot,

why don't you hit me with your best shot

Hit me with your best shot... Fire away[5]

TRUTH OR DARE

I was a new creature in Christ. My old man was deader than dead. I camped out in the secret place. I was untouchable. I dared not even contemplate that I would be sent to prison – not even a thought on my radar – not for a second. The trouble was, I had faith in *my* faith. I had faith that God was going to do it *my* way, in the exact fashion I believed. As this court case dragged out over

---

5 "Hit Me with Your Best Shot"; Lyrics; Edward Schwartz. (As Sung by Pat Benatar)

the next three years, I found out that God's ways were higher than my ways.

"I don't think the way you think. The way you work isn't the way I work." God's Decree. "For as the sky soars high above earth, so the way I work surpasses the way you work, and the way I think is beyond the way you think."

– Isaiah 55:8, MSG

Beloved, do you have faith in your faith, or in the One who has the power to deliver you? The Lord is your Divine Protector! If you are in a trial right now, take comfort in His words to you:

Belle de Jour

Please… My precious flower; fear not,
For I planted you in My garden in a very special spot.
I have enriched the soil under you…
so that you will grow quickly and sturdily into My fullness.
Don't ever fear My child, that I, your loving Father…
will ever fail to attend to you My special flower.
For you will continue to blossom …
as I pour My love out on you.

~Abba Father~

Merrily We Roll Along

As my court case dragged on, I learned to put one foot in front of the other. I acted as if this were already in my rear-view mirror, simply because there was no other option to entertain.

In February 2009, I married Jeff, the love of my life. In 2010, we went to Israel, became certified deliverance ministers through Elijah House, and entered a Word of Faith Bible college. Life was so good! I was living my dream life, with the exception of this bump in the road.

Continuance upon continuance, year after year, this court case dragged on. I knew that I knew that God had a good plan and He was aligning things up in my favor. My prophetic training with Holy Spirit was moving along quickly. I was too busy to notice the bug on my windshield. I could still see straight ahead and nothing could stop me now.

Signs and Wonders
Along the Way

Shortly after I was charged, signs pointing to *no prison* began to happen. A Word of Faith pastor that came to my church occasionally was the first one to speak over me. It was a regular Sunday morning service. He stopped preaching, and all us of a sudden said:

"Whoa! There is someone here that has been charged with financial crimes. But God! He is saying to you this morning; God is going to turn people's hearts towards you. He is going to give you great favor, and you WILL escape the mouth of the lion!"

I could barely contain myself when the Lord said, "Daughter, that word was for you." Yea God! I KNEW that nothing bad was going to happen to me and this was the confirmation.

The next sign I had that there would be no prison time, came from a friend who was pastoring at a nearby church. One day after praying over my court case, she was leaving to take her dogs out for a walk and heard a garbage disposal. She thought to herself, *what was that?* So, she went back into her kitchen to check, but the garbage disposal was not running. Holy Spirit spoke and said; "You just heard MB's case being disposed of." When she shared this with me I was thrilled beyond measure. God was reassuring me once again that I would be delivered.

Another time, I was on the phone with my spiritual mom, Loni. It was before one of my routine court appearances (where I knew would be yet another continuance). As she prayed over me in tongues, the Holy Spirit gave the interpretation. He said;

"Daughter… even though the three Hebrew children went into the fiery furnace (Daniel 3) they knew my arm was not too short to pull them out. Stand until the last second and see My Glory!"

After that I was ecstatic. I now had an inkling of the way God intended to do it. I believed that at my sentencing hearing, the Lord would pull me out. WOW!! What a celebration that would be! I was so looking forward to the day that would happen.

Several months later, I was in our bedroom upstairs and I had a vision. I was standing on a beach and was looking at the sand. All of a sudden, the tide came up and, on its way, out, a vortex opened in the sand. The water and the sand were sucked down into it. I asked Holy Spirit what it meant. He said, "Daughter, what have you been confessing every day?" It was my court case cast into the sea of course, so I knew what He meant. It was Mark 11:23-34, which I had been decreeing:

> "In Jesus name, and upon the authority of His holy word; I speak to my mountain which is this court case; may you be lifted up into the sea and be disposed of. I believe in my heart and do not doubt in my mind, that it will come to pass."

Beloved, I SAW my own case go into the sea. I am here to tell you that His Word is true!

Finally, one day I was on the sofa reading the Word. All of a sudden it was as though a screen dropped behind my eyes and I had a vision. It was of a former landlady who had received a check from me that bounced. In the vision, she was very upset and said the words, *"You've got to be kidding me!"*

I asked the Lord why she was so mad? He answered me and said; *"She is mad at your 33-day violation"*. I thought, *what?* He then led me to the book of Esther. I read where Esther had not been called into the king for thirty days. She then fasted for three days and went boldly to the throne. It was decreed by the royal court that you could not go to the king without being summoned. So, after thirty-three days, Esther violated the order of the court. She asked the king for favor and her wish was granted, and her *"life" was spared.*

So, let me re-cap:

1.) It was prophesied that I would escape the mouth of the lion.

2.) My pastor friend heard audibly, a garbage disposal, meaning that my case was being disposed of.

59

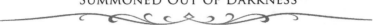

3.) My spiritual mom had an interpretation of tongues that the Lord was going to pull me out of the fiery furnace at the last minute.

4.) I saw my own court case cast into the sea and disposed of in a vision.

5.) I had a vision that confirmed (just like Esther), that I would be given favor by King Jesus by petitioning the throne for help.

Wow. All I can say is that there was never a defendant *so certain* of a good outcome than I was. God had spoken. It was finished.

MY DAY IN COURT

We finally made it. After three years and numerous continuances, the sentencing date was set for August 31st, 2011. I had my entire support system with me. We had made a reservation for twelve at Olive Garden for dinner. This was my big moment! I was going to go before the judge and see the hand of God pluck me out of this, once and for all. Even in the natural, things looked solid. The judge almost always sides with probation's recommendation for sentencing. My pre-sentence investigation report was over-the-top great. It said that I had transformed my life and that prison would serve no purpose.

I was set! My husband Jeff and I went into court that day, surrounded by friends and family. Life could not get any better than this. The judge called me to stand up to receive sentence. It was right out of a scene from "Law and Order." This was so awesome!!! My shining moment had finally come. Everyone was about to see the hand of God work in my life.

The next moment sent shock waves through my body. The judge sentenced me to 40 months in prison. *WHAT???? This can't be!!* I screamed within. What about all the confirmations that I was not going to go to prison? Grief, sorrow and extreme shock ripped through me. I had a visceral reaction and fainted in court.

My attorney somehow convinced the judge to let me go home and surrender myself to the authorities the next morning, to begin serving my sentence. It was the worst night of my Christian walk. I was so sick to my stomach that I could not eat and could barely speak. I was full of dread beyond measure. Mere words cannot describe the grief, shock, and fear I was feeling all at the same time. My life was destroyed in an instant and I wanted to die. It was a miracle that I could even fall asleep, but I did. At 3:11 AM, the Lord woke me up and said these words; "Arise and thresh, oh daughter" I knew the significance of the following scripture in the book Matthew John the Baptist says:

> I indeed baptize you with water unto repentance, but He who is coming after me is mightier than I, whose sandals I am not worthy to carry. He will baptize you with the Holy Spirit **and fire.** – Matthew 3:11, NKJV

Have you ever been besought with grief and fear? Just know that the Lord is with you and His purpose for your testing is not always understood at the time that it is happening. Although the teacher is "quiet" when the student takes the test, remember that He is with you in the fiery furnace.

Crucible

My child, learn from this…

I humbled myself and was obedient to the extreme

all the way to death on the cross because I love you so much,

precious child. You are the apple of My eye.

Know that demons tremble at your obedience.

They tremble at your light.

They love it when you fail.

Thank you for standing fast until the end.

For you are My crucible.[6]

~Your High Priest is interceding for you.~

---

6 Crucible Definition… A container that is subjected to very high temperatures
and pressure; place or occasion of severe test or trial.

PART TWO

To the Oven ...

I stand silently to listen for the one I love,

waiting as long as it takes for the Lord to rescue me.

For God alone has become my Savior.

He alone is my safe place;

His wrap-around presence always protects me.

For He is my champion defender;

there's no risk of failure with God.

So why would I let worry paralyze me,

even when troubles multiply around me?

But look at these who want me dead,

shouting their vicious threats at me!

The moment they discover my weakness

they all begin plotting to take me down.

Liars, hypocrites, with nothing good to say.

All of their energies are spent

on moving me from this exalted place.

– Psalm 62:1-4, TPT –

Chapter 5

SACKCLOTH AND ASHES

Now why do you cry aloud?
Is there no king in your midst? Has your counselor perished?
For pangs have seized you like a woman in labor.
Be in pain, and labor to bring forth,
O daughter of Zion, like a woman in birth pangs.
For now you shall go forth from the city,
You shall dwell in the field, and to Babylon you shall go.
There you shall be delivered;
There the Lord will redeem you From the hand of your enemies.
Now also many nations have gathered against you,
Who say, "Let her be defiled, and let our eye look upon Zion."
But they do not know the thoughts of the Lord,
Nor do they understand His counsel;
For He will gather them like sheaves to the threshing floor.
"Arise and thresh, O daughter of Zion;
For I will make your horn iron,
And I will make your hooves bronze;
You shall beat in pieces many peoples;
I will consecrate their gain to the Lord,
And their substance to the Lord of the whole earth."

– *Micah 4:9-13, NKJV* –

"ARISE AND THRESH, OH DAUGHTER"

*T*he Lord had told me to arise and thresh, but there was no *"arise"* in me. My feet felt like lead, and I could barely walk or speak. The next morning on the way downtown to turn myself into custody, confusion, fear, and anguish ripped through me. I could scarcely breathe.

I was about to hug and kiss my husband for the last time before they took me away in handcuffs. "This can't be happening, God!" I screamed in my head, over and over and over again! A dark cloud engulfed me. I could not hear my Savior's voice, yet I had seen my case go into the sea!!! Where was my Jesus??? *My God, my God... why hast thou forsaken me?*

Heaven was completely silent as they took me away like a common criminal. I was in such grief and agony. Facing prison alone was bad enough, but I could not hear my Beloved's voice. I went from constant fellowship with the Lord, before sentencing, to complete silence.

> *But not a word was spoken, the church bells all were broken.*
> *And the three men I admire most...*
>
> *the Father, Son, and the Holy Ghost,*
> *They caught the last train for the coast, the day the music died.*[7]

WELCOME TO THE JUNGLE

I had to sit in the local county jail for one week before being transported to prison. My first day locked up was almost more than

---

7 "American Pie"; Lyrics by Don Mclean. (As sung by Don McClean)

I could bear. Mostly, I was in with prostitutes and women that had been arrested for drunk driving. I cried out to Jesus and sobbed me a river. I begged for the peace of God to come, but it did not. My comforter was nowhere to be found.

"I don't belong here! How can this be?" I cried. I called Jeff as often as I could use the phone, but he was helpless to do anything. We felt destroyed. Jeff had lost his first wife to alcoholism, and now he was losing me to prison. How could a loving God allow this to happen? What about all those confirmations I had received about not going to prison?

Every day in despair I called my spiritual mom, Loni, and I would always ask the same thing. "Has God said anything to you about me yet?" She would say, "No, honey I am sorry." This was inconceivable to me. I needed to hear from God, and He was not speaking.

I knew that the Word says that *He will never leave us nor forsake us*, but now I even doubted that. I felt forsaken, abandoned and spiritually gutted. I was in deep grief, and there seemed no way out. I was shattered into a million pieces. My heart was broken, and there was no light at the end of the tunnel.

Beloved, have you ever felt like God has forsaken you? If you have or do right now, know that He has NOT! His word is true. Even in the darkest places, He is with you. King David knew this all too well when he wrote:

Where can I go from Your Spirit? Or where can I flee from
Your presence?
If I ascend into heaven, You are there; If I make my bed in
hell, behold, You are there.
If I take the wings of the morning,

And dwell in the uttermost parts of the sea,
Even there Your hand shall lead me, And Your right hand
shall hold me.
If I say, "Surely the darkness shall fall on me," Even the night
shall be light about me;
Indeed, the darkness shall not hide from You,
but the night shines as the day;
The darkness and the light are both alike to You.

– Psalm 139:7-12, NKJV

Once I arrived at the prison, I was labeled an offender. That is how I was addressed – "Offender." My shame and humiliation had only just begun. The definition of an offender is: *wrongdoer, criminal, lawbreaker, miscreant, malefactor, felon, delinquent, culprit, guilty party, outlaw, sinner, transgressor; malfeasant.*

I *knew* in my heart that I was none of those things, but what my heart *felt* was very different. Heaven had shut over me, and I was completely alone. In prison, I no longer had a husband to comfort and protect me. I feared for my safety. How could God protect me? His presence seemed nowhere to be found.

I was stripped of all my freedoms – When to get up and when to go to bed, even choosing what food to put in my body, who my roommate was, and what I did for work. And these are only a few things; this entire book could be about everything I lost in prison. My life as I knew it was over. I lost my marital bed, my friends, my family and my church in a nano-second. Gone…all gone. Poof! I was hanging on to my sanity for dear life. For the first time in my Christian walk, I felt utterly hopeless and defeated. I went through the motions of each day in a dark trance.

My first job in prison was to do unit maintenance (cleaning). I worked for a sadistic guard with OCD who hated women. He would make me get on my hands and knees and scrub underneath the furnace in a boiler room that nobody ever saw or went to. He would constantly berate and verbally abuse the other women and me. The Bible says in Romans 13:1-2 to submit to governing authorities *so it will go well for you.* I could not fathom that this was applicable to my situation, but I did it, anyway, because I knew that I was to be obedient to the Word of God at all costs. My obedience was being tested, and I was living my worst nightmare.

Every day I woke up with same question; "Why, God, why? How could this happen to me, the daughter you love? How could all those prophetic confirmations of *no prison* have not come true?" My answer did not come for eight months.

ABOUT MY FATHER'S BUSINESS

They say that the worst thing about hell is that you are *separated* from the Living God. After literally living in what seemed like hell for two months, the moment I was waiting for finally arrived. God spoke!

It was an October morning just like every other morning. I opened my eyes and heard the following words; *"Daughter, take off the sackcloth and ashes, it's time to be about My business."*

My heart almost came out of my chest! "GOD IS ALIVE!!!! I can breathe again! He loves me, He loves me!"

Beloved, have you ever felt that you are all alone and that God has abandoned you?

Be strong and of good courage, do not fear nor be afraid of them (The enemy); for the Lord your God, He is the One who goes with you. He will not leave you nor forsake you. –Deuteronomy 31:6, NKJV

If you are in a place where you feel abandoned by God, let me assure you of this. He has not abandoned you! This is truly what He is saying to you in this moment:

Rivers of Loving Glory

Peace be still, My child.

For Rivers of Loving Glory will heal you from all hurts.

Come to Me in the night and experience the light of My presence.

I will bathe you and nourish you with My love.

My Oil of Gladness is bestowed unto you!

Fruitfulness, faithfulness, patience, loving-kindness, authority,

and matchless grace are all yours, My precious one.

I burn with love for you!

~Lion of Judah~

There was a new spring in my step and I no longer felt alone. My Comforter had come, and I could bear anything with Him at my side! I am a living testimony that you can do ALL things through Christ who strengthens you! (Philippians 4:13) Within the prison walls, I went about my Father's business with vigor. While serving

my time there, I cast out demons, laid hands on the sick and they recovered. The devil was under my feet and I led many women who needed Jesus and salvation to Christ.

> He has given me a new song to sing, a hymn of praise
> to our God. Many will see what he has done and be amazed.
> They will put their trust in the Lord. –Psalm 40:3, NLT

The next few months were amazing. I dug deep and found the joy of the Lord. I had been transferred to become a mopper in the prison's kitchen. In the natural, it does not sound like a promotion, but it was. I was no longer under the authority of the sadistic guard. I now wore two name tags; one said "Offender" and the other one said "Mopper."

Ask me if I cared? I did not. Small victories were huge blessings! I was so grateful to my King for delivering me out of one job and into another. Are you grateful for something today that is small? Think big! God is the God of the breakthrough!

You might ask yourself, how could she find unspeakable joy mopping in a women's prison kitchen? Beloved… happiness is based on someone's circumstances, but joy is a fruit of the Spirit. One day I caught myself dancing with my mop and singing praises to my King. (Selah) Dig deep friends, for *the joy of the Lord is your strength.*

> The Lord is my strength and my shield; my heart trusted in
> Him, and I am helped;
> Therefore my heart greatly rejoices, and with my song I will
> praise Him – Psalm 28:7, NKJV

One of the benefits of pressing into the Lord is that no matter what is happening around you, you remain sequestered in the secret place, under the covering of His divine protection. A fight broke out one day in the cafeteria, and the guards swarmed the two girls with their cans of mace. When the mace was released, numerous tables cleared on either side of me. Women were screaming, gasping and clawing at their eyes. Not me though. I sat there protected with an angel standing guard over me, eating my mashed potatoes. NOTHING could touch me, because I was in "God's Witness Protection Program." The word says, "The angel of the Lord encamps about those who fear Him" (Psalm 34:7; NKJV)

About that time one week later, I saw the same angel standing watch over me when I was at work. He had to be at least 15 feet tall. He was wearing a light blue gown and had a gold sash over his shoulder. I knew that I knew, that my God had such an amazing hedge around me. I was safe, and I was oh so loved.

O God, hear my prayer. Listen to my heart's cry. For no matter where I am, even when I'm far from home, I will cry out to You for a Father's help. When I'm feeble and overwhelmed by life, guide me into Your glory, where I am safe and sheltered. Lord, You are a paradise of protection to me. You lift me high above the fray. None of my foes can touch me when I'm held firmly in Your wrap-around presence! Keep me in this glory. Let me live continually under Your splendor-shadow, hiding my life in You forever.

– Psalm 61:1-4, TPT

FROM POINT A TO POINT B

After the revelation of the Lord's divine protection over me there, I experienced another major victory. I had applied for and was received into the Christian women's program called IFI (Inner-Change Freedom Initiative). I was moved into a different housing unit where I would be among other Christian women who were being taught the Bible. I thought to myself, *it's only uphill from here!*

I thought wrong. The warfare in that unit was so intense it was suffocating. I ended up with a severely demonically oppressed room-mate who had murdered her husband. She was an extremely large African-American woman who ruled the roost. On my first day as her roommate, she told me that she slept during the day on the weekends. She instructed me that all the blinds in the room were to remain shut or else! No light was to be allowed in the room, nor could I make any noise, so she could sleep.

When my room was dark, a demonic spirit of fear hovered in that room. I slept with one eye open and was even afraid to shower for fear that I would wake her up and get beat up. Emotionally, I was living a double life. On the one hand, I knew that was in the secret place, yet at night I felt fear. But God! He proved me wrong. Once again, He showed me that His word is true. One night as I lay in bed with tears running down my face, Jesus came into the room. He said to me gently, "Come here!" and he held me in His loving arms. I felt peace in the midst of the storm. I was not alone, and I knew my Protector was with me.

That encounter gave me a boldness that I had never felt before, so I made my move. I led my roommate to Christ and ministered the baptism in the Holy Spirit to her. At night, we would then pray together before going to bed. The King of Mercy had come in. All glory to King Jesus! What a transformation!

Things were running along smoothly as I went about my Father's business, *so I thought*. I was praying for the women at night and ministering to them the baptism in the Holy Spirit, and the atmosphere was shifting for the good. But then the director of IFI became offended at me. She called me in to her office and informed me she felt IFI was not a good "fit" for me and that I had to leave the program. I found out later that she felt I was "taking control" over her program. She told me that these ladies could barely drink milk, and how dare I give them meat to eat. Wow; enough said. I was flourishing in my assignment in prison and now I was being rejected. How many more surprises could I take? I was about to find out.

I was informed that I would now become a math tutor. God has a sense of humor. I was in prison for a financial crime and yet now He was placing me in position as a math tutor. This meant that I was being sent to live in the educational unit. It was known in prison as the "hood" because most of the women there were uneducated and were going to school for their GEDs. I had to repent for believing the lie that this place was the hood. These women were precious to God, they just didn't know it yet.

I was feeling rejected and dejected as I pulled my wagon with all my possessions from the IFI living unit to the other. With tears streaming down my face, I cried out to the Lord and asked Him again, "Why, God, why?" He said; "*I hardened Pharaoh's heart, didn't I?*" It then struck me. It was His will that I was leaving IFI and was on to my next assignment. Have you ever been plucked out of your circumstances? If so, it is crucial to always remember the following scripture:

> And we know that all things work together for good to those who love God, to those who are the called according to His purpose. – Romans 8:28, NKJV

I hope this encourages you as it is one of my favorite passages from the Book of Psalms. I named it "My Prison Woes Psalm":

> Keep me safe, O mighty God. I run for dear life to You, my safe place.
>
> So I said to the Lord God, "You are my Maker, my Mediator, and my Master. Any good thing You find in me has come from You."
>
> Yet there are those who yield to their weakness, and they will have troubles and sorrows unending. I never gather with such ones, nor give them honor in any way.
>
> Lord, I have chosen You alone as my inheritance. You are my prize, my pleasure, and my portion. I leave my destiny and its timing in Your hands.
>
> The way You counsel and correct me makes me praise You more, for Your whispers in the night give me wisdom, showing me what to do next.
>
> Because You are close to me and always available, my confidence will never be shaken, for I experience Your wraparound presence every moment.
>
> – Psalm 16: 1-2, 4-8, NKJV

Chapter 6

A Lonely Little Petunia in an Onion Patch

I'm a lonely little petunia in an onion patch,
an onion patch, an onion patch.
I'm a lonely little petunia in an onion patch,
and all I do is cry all day.
Boo hoo! Boo hoo!
The air is so strong, it takes my breath away.
I'm a lonely little petunia in an onion patch,
Oh won't you come and play with me?
He put me in this bed, I'll bet his face is red. (The devil)
I call him down with every teardrop that I shed.
If I only had him here, I'd take him by the ear
And make him share my misery.[8]

---

8 "I'm a Lonely Little Petunia in an Onion Patch"; Songwriters Maurie Hartman, John Kamano, & Billy Faber. (As sung by Richard Perlmutter)

I SURRENDER ALL

*T*was a lonely little petunia in an onion patch. That's how I felt starting over again in a new building with new people and with new guards. I knew God had allowed me to go to prison, and now this move to a new building... but it was the enemy who ultimately was responsible for all of this. Before I knew Jesus, the enemy came to kill, steal and destroy my life and almost succeeded. I blame him for the mess that landed me in prison. Therefore, I will spend the rest of my days giving him a black eye! I have asked the Lord for a ring-side seat when they throw him into the lake of fire. (Smile) Does anyone wish to join me?

As I walked into the new building, you could have heard a pin drop. I was on foreign soil now, in a land I did not know. My white skin made me a minority. I felt like an intruder who had stumbled into an enemy camp.

I had been promoted to be a math tutor, and these were my new students. My mind screamed again, "Why, God why?" He did not answer me. I made my way to the front desk, and a beautiful middle-aged blonde guard checked me in. I felt an instant connection to her compassion and warmth. I later found out she was a Christian, and that place was her ministry. *God is sure full of surprises*, I thought. I was not sure of how many more God surprises I could take.

As I look back, I see how God used this relocation to the educational unit as a catalyst to make His move on my heart. One day as I was getting comfortable in my new surroundings, He spoke. He said, *"Daughter, I had to get you out of the world, to get the world out of you.*" He would often send the following song to me, and now, more than ever, the meaning became clear.

> *How do you solve a problem like Maria?*
>
> *How do you catch a cloud and pin it down?*
>
> *How do you find a word that means Maria?*
>
> *A flibbertigibbet! A will-o'-the wisp! A clown!*
>
> *Many a thing you know you'd like to tell her.*
>
> *Many a thing she ought to understand*
>
> *But how do you make her stay and listen to all you say?*
>
> *How do you keep a wave upon the sand?*
>
> *Oh, how do you solve a problem like Maria?*
>
> *How do you hold a moonbeam in your hand?*[9]

It made perfect sense. Nowhere to run and nowhere to hide. Just me and Him. No cell phone and no television. It had to be supernatural for me to not even want to escape into television, as most of the inmates had them in their rooms. Upon hearing the statement about getting the world out of me, the desire to watch TV or read the newspaper left in an instant. Poof!

Have you ever had a touch from God change your heart in a moment? I hope this word ministers to you right now, where you are at:

---

9 "Maria"; From the musical, "The Sound of Music," Songwriters; Richard Rogers & Oscar Hammerstein. (As sung by Julie Andrews)

Apple of My Eye

My Liebchen; ("My Little Love")
You are the apple of My eye
and I am fiercely devoted to you!
I wish to consume every fiber of your being.
Come to me and wave the white flag of surrender
to the things of this world.
They are meaningless and have no earthly value.
I crave your fellowship!

~Your Adoring King~

After that revelation, I started pressing into Him and His Word even more. I was like a "word-sponge." I could not wait to get to bed so I could get up and read the Word! The more I read, the more I had to have. I absolutely had to have the Word or I would die! I was falling even more radically in love with my Lord.

He was my Living Bread and His Word was essential for me to live. Through this season, I was learning to be content in my circumstances. I came to know an intimacy with my Jesus in a greater measure I had not known before. I now understand what the Apostle Paul meant when he wrote:

I know how to be abased, and I know how to abound.
Everywhere and in all things, I have learned both to be full
and to be hungry, both to abound and to suffer need.

– Philippians 4:12

I say this jokingly, but God did a number on my marriage too.
Jeff came to visit me at least three times a week. There were no dis-
tractions that so often afflict marriages. All we did was talk. We sat
across from each other and just talked. How many times do married couples do that today? It was bittersweet. I had been taken
out of my marital bed and had temporarily lost physical intimacy,
but my marriage was climbing higher and higher into emotional
intimacy. I am not sure I would have that level today if I had not
spent all those hours talking to Jeff. Another example of Romans
8:28 in action.

HOLY SPIRIT UNIVERSITY

One thing I know for sure is that God is in control. He arranged
for me to have a roommate that left for work as I was coming home
from my shift at school. Class was now in session, and my Teacher
was always ready with the day's lesson. I called these sessions, "Flash
Cards 101."

Holy Spirit would show me a flash vision and then He would
either give me a corresponding scripture, lyrics to a song that matched
the vision, or would speak to me what was hidden in the vision. For
example; one time He gave me a vision of the Minnesota Vikings
in a team huddle. I then heard their fight song in my head. It wasn't
about the Vikings, rather it was about Holy Spirit coaching me

regarding different ways that He would speak to me, moving forward. This education was priceless, and the good news was that there was no student loan that needed to be paid off.

MY PROFESSORS

My professors were the Old Testament prophets. Holy Spirit would not let me out of their classes no matter how much I tried. *Oh no, not Ezekiel again!* Actually, the Lord took me through Ezekiel's temple vision, and it was spectacular. I am not going to get into what He showed me and why, except to say that the Lord is very serious about the ordinances of His Temple.

By this time, I was spending at least four to six hours a day in the Word, and it was *the best of times and the worst of times.* It was such an exhilarating feeling to lose myself in the Word, all the while sitting in prison with no freedoms. As the song says; "Just a spoonful of sugar, makes the medicine go down." Jesus was the sugar, and I was addicted to that sugar! I encourage you to press in to Jesus through His Word if you are in the wilderness right now. As you do, not only will you find comfort, He will start unveiling His truths for your life.

It was through Ezekiel 3:4-5 that He revealed to me my calling. The moment after I read this scripture, I knew my ministry. Fire came down from heaven and breathed on this verse. My ministry would be to the church whose speech I was familiar with and not the outside world. I was to minister *to* the Body of Christ.

Then He said to me: "Son of man, go to the house of Israel and speak with My words to them. For you are not sent to a people of *unfamiliar speech* and of hard language, but to the house of Israel." – Ezekiel 3:4-5, NKJV

I had taken on the mantle of "Overcomer," and broken Christians needed to know that with the Lord on their side; they could maneuver any minefield in life that they needed to cross. One of the reasons I have written this book is to encourage you, friend. With God on your side, you cannot fail!

Still… day after day, after day, I would wake up and ask the Lord the same question; "Lord, what about all the prophetic words and signs I would not go to prison?" I still believed that I would get a supernatural miracle like Peter and walk out of prison. But at this point He would only answer me with a song. I would often call Loni and ask her what the Lord was saying. She finally said one day that He had spoken. He said that I (MB); was the miracle. I was like *WHAT???? What does He mean, I am the miracle? I want out of here!*

After hearing the following song over and over, I finally got it. I WAS the miracle. God was changing me from the inside out. The great heart surgeon was stealthy at work, ever gently cutting away things that I was so desperately trying to hang on to. Now I knew why He gave me this song that played continually in my head:

(Me):

There have been times in my life,

I've been wondering why.

Still, somehow, I believed I'd always survive.

Now, I'm not so sure.

(Holy Spirit):
You think that maybe it's over, only if you want it to be.
Are you going to wait for a sign, your miracle?
Stand up and fight!
This is it, make no mistake where you are.
Your back's to the corner, the waiting is over,
No, don't you run, no way to hide,
no time for wondering why.
It's here, the moment is now, about to decide.
Keep Me near her in your heart.
Know whatever you do, I am here by your side .[10]

Beloved, I know that it's not always an easy walk down the road of destiny. I pray as you read the following passage that you will find comfort. Even David, on his way to becoming king, cried out to the Lord when he was discouraged in the wilderness. This is how I often felt in prison:

Lord, I'm fading away. I'm discouraged and lying in the dust; revive me by Your word, just like you promised You would.

I've poured out my life before You, and You've always been there for me. So now I ask: teach me more of Your holy decrees.

Open up my understanding to the ways of Your wisdom and I will meditate deeply on Your splendor and Your wonders.

My life's strength melts away with grief and sadness; come strengthen me and encourage me with Your words.

---

10 "This is It"; Songwriters; Kenny Loggins & Michael McDonald. (As sung by Kenny Loggins)

Keep me far away from what is false; give me grace to stay true to Your laws. – Psalm 119:25-29, TPT

Friend, God's destiny for your life is matchless and secured in Heaven! All you need to do is walk in obedience to His Word. Please take comfort in this knowledge.

Drenched in His Favor

Make no mistake about it, My precious saint…
I have bred you for greatness!
Circumcised thy heart to the things of this world.
Watch Me catapult you into a realm of endless possibilities.
Your destiny is secure. Your authority is matchless.
Abide in Me and be true to yourself!
You are anointed to do battle with the kingdom of darkness!
You are drenched in My favor.

~Spirit of the Living God~

A LIGHT AT THE END OF THE TUNNEL

No one told me about the existence of a program called Boot Camp until I was already serving my time in prison. I later found out that my attorney didn't even know about it. Boot Camp was a 180-day program for non-violent offenders. Once you completed successfully, you would get released early from prison. All you had to do was train for the physical tests required to get in, and pass them. At age 54, it looked grim. All of the squads that were going were comprised of women in their 20s and 30s. But with God ALL things are possible (Luke 1:37).

So, I set my course before me, and I trained and trained. The day came for me to take my tests. The odds were against me, but hey, if Elijah could outrun Ahab's chariot under the spirit of "counsel and might" (1 Kings 18:46), I could pass these tests and endure the physical challenges of boot camp.

The day came and I passed my tests. Oh, what a glorious day! This was God's doing, and it was marvelous in my eyes. I also had to get a physical from the prison doctor to clear me to go. He asked me several times; "Are you sure you think you can do this?" I answered him with an enthusiastic "YES, SIR!" Nothing could stop me now. There was a light at the end of my tunnel, and my hope-filled heart was on top of the world! I had such hope! I knew I would be home soon and that my God had made way for me to prosper in the wilderness.

Chapter 7

THE BIG REVEAL

MB had a little Lamb; whose fleece was white as snow.
And everywhere that MB went, the Lamb was sure to go.
It followed her to school (Prison) one day
which was against the rules.
It made the women laugh and play, to see a Lamb at school.
And so, the teacher turned it out, but still it lingered near,
And waited patiently about, till MB did appear.
"Why does the Lamb love MB so?" the eager children cry.
"Why, MB loves the Lamb, you know." the teacher did reply.[11]

EYES ON HOME PLATE

With the knowledge that I was going to boot camp, I felt like I was standing on third base with my eyes on home plate. "Can I steal this base, God, when no one is looking?" I asked. He said, "No, daughter, you must run this last leg race with endurance."

---

11 An adaptation of "Mary Had a Little Lamb," a poem by Sarah Josepha Hale

I had heard horror stories from women who had returned back to the prison from boot camp. They either could not "cut it" with the intense physical demands, or they had not complied with the strict requirements of the program.

Rumors abounded about boot camp. The naysayers thought I couldn't make it. I was 54 at the time, and in the natural, it looked daunting. BUT God! His Word said I could make it!

> But those who wait on the Lord,
> Shall renew their strength;
> They shall mount up with wings like eagles,
> They shall run and not be weary,
> They shall walk and not faint.
> —Isaiah 40:31, NKJV

I had also heard a rumor that in boot camp, your routine was so structured from sunup to sundown, that there was no time to read the Bible. I panicked. WHAT? How could I get through my day with no Word? Perish the thought! But my focus was on Christ in me, the hope of glory (Colossians 1:27). He was in me and I in Him, and without Him I could do nothing. I knew my spirit was soaked in His word and that the Comforter would minister to me as I went throughout my days up there.

Do you need a reminder of His faithfulness towards you? This is for you!

Faithful and True

I am putting a new song in your heart.

It is the Song of the Ancients.

For I am coming on a white horse in power and might!

I AM He who is called Faithful and True.

Circumcise thy heart to the things of this world, My child.

Relegate an impoverished mind.

Be quickened in your spirit to My voice.

Redemption is Mine saith the Lord…

And I will smack you down with the power of My love!

A side note. One day while abiding in Him, before beginning the boot camp program, I was correcting math papers. All of a sudden, He translated me to the Whole Foods parking lot in my city. One minute I was at my desk, and the next minute, I was standing in the parking lot at Whole Foods. Why did He do that? I think He was showing me what He was going to do with me in the future. It was a demonstration of His mighty power.

One of the benefits of boot camp was that I would no longer be strip-searched every time I had a visitor. Being strip-searched was awful and humiliating beyond measure. I had to go through it every time after someone came to see me. I learned to shift my focus not on what was coming at the end of each visit, but rather to stay present in the moment during my visits. It was difficult to do, but it was another victory that I overcame in prison. If we are stuck in the past, we cannot move forward. If we are worried about the future, we are not present in the moment.

Friend of God, like me, you can overcome anything because Holy Spirit has equipped you! Even though I was called an offender, stripped searched six to ten times a week, and had no freedom in the natural, I WAS free. Freer than I had ever been, free in Jesus, and my spirit soared. Friend of God, it's time to get lost in Jesus and His Word. He is inviting you to press in to Him further and further.

Your Fire Pleases Me

Come dine at My table…

for a rich banquet awaits thee.

Come experience the bounty of My goodness.

Heavenly rewards rain down on you,

My precious child,

and I ravish you with My love.

Your fire pleases Me!

~Christ the King~

LEAN NOT TO YOUR OWN UNDERSTANDING

As I shared before, I was constantly asking the Lord about how I could have ended up in prison, after I had received so many prophetic confirmations that I was not going to go there. He never revealed the answer to me, until a cold March day in 2012. Whether He answered or not, though, I was faithful to love Him, press into Him and to serve Him. That being said… I was not about to stop asking.

I had been in prison now for eight months, and boot camp was in my near future. Six months more to go, and I would be home for good. I could barely contain my excitement. God had prepared my heart and I was ready to come home.

I knew the road ahead would be challenging, but I was ready. The Lord had spoken to my spiritual mom Loni about boot camp. He told her that upon completion of boot camp I would have confidence in my ability to get through anything. Let me explain that. I already had confidence "in Him," but this challenge was to instill confidence in myself, my physical abilities, my willingness to follow orders completely, and other attributes of being a good soldier. He also told her that boot camp would be beneficial to me in the future.

One day He said to me; *"Make sure you read the book!"* I looked at my extensive book collection and asked, "What book?" He did not answer me. The next day I was called down to property to pick up a package. As the officer handed it to me, the Lord said, *This is the book.* I opened it up with great excitement. It was titled, *Growing in the Prophetic,* by Mike Bickle (IHOP, Kansas City).

I could not WAIT to get back to my room after dinner to read the book! It had to be one of the longest days in prison in the recent months that I could remember. Not in a bad way, though; I knew that my Father had something to reveal to me, and I was like a child at Christmas. I had been given a gift from my Daddy and could not wait to "unwrap" the revelation He wanted me to have.

I have to thank my precious husband Jeff for his faithfulness to obey the voice of God in sending me the book. I could write an entire chapter on the gratitude I have to the Lord for bringing me the man of my dreams. Ours was a covenant marriage with Jesus in the center, and I was so thankful for this man of God. If you are reading this book and were one of the people that reached out to Jeff in my absence, I thank you from the bottom of my heart.

Although different in so many ways, not for a moment, do I diminish the fact that Jeff's hardship was equal to mine. Every evening he came home to an empty house. He went to bed alone and ate meals alone. He had been left behind, yet he was my biggest champion. He was so faithful to send me his teaching notes from church every week so that I could keep up with my church and pastor Mac's teachings. So, thank you, honey. You are my love, and I adore you.

3 STEPS IN PROPHECY

After dinner that night I raced to my room. I opened the book and read through the first few chapters. I was hanging on every word! Although many of these things I already knew, I was confident that my Father had something *in particular* He wanted to show me.

At the beginning of the book, the author stated that there were three phases to the prophetic:

1.) Receiving the divine information, no matter whatever form it comes (Audible, dream, vision, impression or still small voice)

2.) Interpreting the divine information as to what it's about

3.) Applying the divine information to the receiver's life

It stressed the utmost extreme importance of the *application* of the divine revelation. People who receive wrongly applied revelation can become wounded. It could be that either the prophecy caused great confusion, or because it never came to pass.

Mike gave the example of a man who received a word that he was going to prosper as a musician and become an integral member of a worship team. In fact, the man owned a music store. The immature prophet had seen musical notes over the man as he prophesied and falsely discerned out of his flesh.

The office of prophet is not to be taken lightly, but rather reverently and humbly, properly discerning the truth through Holy Spirit and not one's flesh. The urge to get ahead of God and speak out of the flesh must be avoided at all costs.

After reading and meditating on those three phases of the prophetic, it was time to go to bed. I could not wait to wake up and see all that my Father had for me! It was a miracle I could even fall asleep, I was so excited. Nothing prepared my heart though, for what I woke up to the next morning.

HOPE DEFERRED MAKES THE HEART SICK

The second my eyes opened up, the Lord said; "*Hope deferred makes the heart sick.*" I felt a crushing blow to my heart. All my hope in the promises of boot camp left, as fear raced through my veins like ice-cold water. I had not panicked like that since being sentenced to prison.

"OH NO!!!!! Lord, please don't take boot camp from me!" My hope was in going to boot camp, and now I believed my hope was going to be deferred. He and I both knew that if He asked me not to go, I would be obedient and say yes.

That would mean that He had a purpose for me to serve out the full length of my sentence. My heart raced and I could not eat nor speak. Breakfast was mandatory, and I trudged down to the lunchroom like a zombie. I was full of dread as I waited for the question to come, but His request never came. When I got back from breakfast, all I could do was frantically pace the room like a caged animal. I couldn't breathe! Wait! It was my turn to walk outside! They scheduled outside time by the first letter of your last name, so I grabbed my coat and went outside to the courtyard. I walked and cried, and walked and cried.

I had put my music headset on and was listening to Christian music, hoping to drown out the noise inside my head. All of a sudden, the music stopped and the moment came when the Lord spoke to me. I overheard Him ask Satan the same question He asked in Job 1:8:

Then the Lord said to Satan, "Have you considered My servant Job, that there is none like him on the earth, a blameless and upright man, one who fears God and shuns evil?"

94

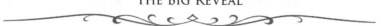

Except this time, it was my name in that question. I heard Him say; *"Have you considered My servant MB?"* I felt like I was struck by lightning and I fell to my knees. You mean this has all been a test, My Lord? I was speechless, yet I had a million questions.

I went back to my room on auto-pilot and waited for His fire to fall upon my heart. There was no need to ask Him anything, because He knew my questions before I did, as He is omniscient/all-knowing. I sat on the bed and waited for Him to speak.

A Conversation with My Father

Abba… *"Hope deferred makes the hearts sick, doesn't it, daughter?"*

Me… "Yes, Lord."

Abba… *"Let me ask you some questions. Am I not your Father, and do I not watch over My word to perform it in your life?"*

Me… "Yes, Lord."

Abba… *"Where do you need be, to escape the mouth of the Lion?"*

Me… "Right here, in the lion's den."

Abba… *"Have you not, like Esther, come boldly to the throne of grace in this place every day, and I have I not given you favor?"*

Me… "Yes Daddy"

Abba… *"My arm is not too short to pull you out to go to boot camp, now is it?"*

Me… "No, it is not."

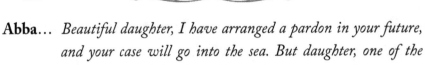
Abba… *Beautiful daughter, I have arranged a pardon in your future, and your case will go into the sea. But daughter, one of the things you needed to learn from your prison experience was to experience how it feels when prophecy is misapplied in your life, and you did it to yourself.*

*You see…. You took all of those prophecies and determined that they had to do with you not going to prison, when in fact, I have fulfilled all (but one), of them while you were "**In**" prison.*

I know you suffered great pain, but it was necessary to equip you in your calling. For if you are to stand in My office of prophet, and prophesy over My children; you better get it right.

I needed to teach you the danger of misapplying a prophecy over someone's life. Because if you do, wounding can occur, and there is a danger of them turning from Me.

WOW! WOW! WOW! My questions were finally answered. Revelation flooded my spirit and I wept at the sovereignty and mercy of God. Yes, the mercy of God. I then realized that this trial was to equip me as a prophet. I was to only say what I heard my Father say and to do only what I saw my Father do. In the Father's GREAT love for His children, (that I would prophesy over) He allowed me to suffer Like Job, in order to show me the danger of misapplying His words. Let me clarify: God did not lie to me (God is not a man that He should lie – Numbers 23:19) but when I – and even others – misinterpreted the words and signs He gave, He did not intervene to correct. It was a hard but necessary lesson. In Wendy Alec's book, *Revealing Heaven*, she discusses the great sifting of the saints. I highly recommend this book. John Paul Jackson also taught on the "Dark Night of the Soul."

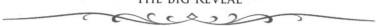

Jesus said,

[Discipleship Is Costly] Then Jesus said to His disciples, "If anyone wishes to follow Me [as My disciple], he must deny himself [set aside selfish interests], and take up his cross [expressing a willingness to endure whatever may come] and follow Me [believing in Me, conforming to My example in living and, if need be, suffering or perhaps dying because of faith in Me]." – Matthew 16:24, AMP

Can I get a witness? Properly stewarding the calling He has given you is of utmost importance to Him. So much so… in His love, that He allows us to be refined in the fire, in order to raise us up to new heights. All for the Glory of King Jesus and Him alone!

A SPOONFUL OF SUGAR MAKES THE MEDICINE GO DOWN

Through all of this, I discovered two sides to the God coin. One side is grace, favor, and blessing, and the flip side is trial, suffering, and testing. So many churches today preach only one side of the God coin. They are seeker-friendly churches only looking to fill seats in their congregation. They do not teach the full counsel of God and that God does allow us to be tested in the wilderness, as Jesus was in Luke 4:1:

Then Jesus, being filled with the Holy Spirit, returned from the Jordan and was led by the Spirit into the wilderness.

Beloved, if you are being tested by the Lord right now, may you find comfort in the following word from His heart to yours.

Chastened in Love

I have chastened you, My child,
So that you would not be ignorant of the enemy's devices.
An abundance of joy and an abundance of oil
poured out to you in My presence.
Seek Me freely and liberally I will bestow to you
a blessing you cannot contain.
Extravagant love through extravagant worship
is what I desire.
I see you in the secret place.
You abide in Me... your fire pleases Me

~Spirit of the Living God~

After the revelation of why God allowed me to go to prison, I knew what had to be done. I needed to focus on my future. The Lord told me that my trajectory was pointed due north and I knew what it meant.

In the natural, I was headed north up to the Canadian border for boot camp. In the spiritual, I knew that once I got back home, I would be catapulted to the north side of the Holy of Holies where the Table of Shewbread was. I was to eat bread in the presence of Lord and feed it to His children. The following word describes Heaven as being in the north.

He comes from the north as golden splendor; with God is awesome majesty. – Job 37:22, NKJV

Chapter 8

THE THRESHING FLOOR IN A FOREIGN LAND

When you wish upon a star,

makes no difference who you are.

Anything your heart desires will come to you,

If your heart is in your dream,

no request is too extreme. [12]

THROUGH THE LOOKING GLASS

The trip to Togo, Minnesota, where the boot camp was held, was amazing. God's country all the way. It was May 2012, so spring was in the air and the scenery was breathtaking. My new squad and I rode up in a van and even stopped at a McDonalds for lunch. I was given a taste of freedom for the first time in almost a year. My McDonalds hamburger tasted like manna from Heaven and the living was easy… or so I thought.

---

12 "When You Wish Upon a Star"; Songwriters: Leigh Harline / Ned Washington. (As sung by Cliff Edwards)

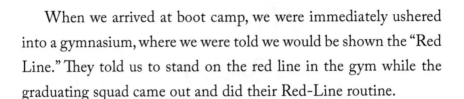

When we arrived at boot camp, we were immediately ushered into a gymnasium, where we were told we would be shown the "Red Line." They told us to stand on the red line in the gym while the graduating squad came out and did their Red-Line routine.

All of a sudden, the graduating squad starting marching in formation and yelling cadences. I swear I thought I was looking at a West Point group of cadets. Their formation and routine were awesome and frightening at the same time. *Dear God, how am I supposed to learn how to do this?* I was weak in the knees and all I could think was, "Toto, we're not in Kansas anymore." The rest of the day we were shown the barracks and told what our expectations, duties and daily routines were going to be. From sunup to sundown there was literally no rest. You were either marching, doing manual labor or in class.

Some of the officers were former National Guard, and they ran this camp to military specifications. I was floored. *God, I can't do this. I'm 54 and my body can't take this!* He said, *"Daughter…be still and know that I am God. Your acacia wood is strong!"* I knew what He meant – acacia wood was what the Ark of the Covenant was made of. I was His ark that carried His presence.

THE FLOOD PLAIN OF THE JORDAN

If you have run with the footmen, and they have wearied you, then how can you contend with horses? And if in the land of peace, in which you trusted, they wearied you, then how will you do in the floodplain of the Jordan?

– Jeremiah 12:5, NKJV

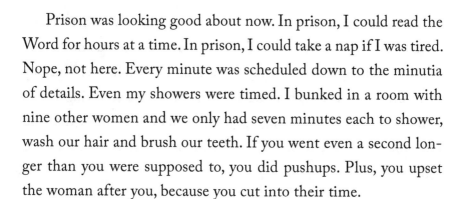

Prison was looking good about now. In prison, I could read the Word for hours at a time. In prison, I could take a nap if I was tired. Nope, not here. Every minute was scheduled down to the minutia of details. Even my showers were timed. I bunked in a room with nine other women and we only had seven minutes each to shower, wash our hair and brush our teeth. If you went even a second longer than you were supposed to, you did pushups. Plus, you upset the woman after you, because you cut into their time.

The very first time I showered, I panicked that I would not get done in time. In my haste, I dropped both my shampoo and conditioner bottles on top of my feet. I had such serious bruising and swelling on the top of my feet, that they even considered taking me to the ER in the next town. I had to march in military-issue marching boots everywhere I went, and the pain was excruciating. After you showered, you had 10 minutes to make your bed to military specs. (Yes, a quarter had to be flipped on your bed.) They also measured the cuff-on the rolldown of the blanket. If you were over 4 inches, even a 1/8 of an inch, you did pushups.

The enemy swooped in and badgered me constantly with the same thought. *You're not going to make it. You're not going to make it. You're not going to make it!* The enemy himself was hazing me and was ruthless in his pursuit of me. I was scared out of my mind and he took full advantage.

Your uniform had to be perfect too. You did your own laundry and had to iron everything with absolutely no wrinkles, or you did pushups. I got up earlier than everyone else on Saturdays just to make sure I had ample time to iron my uniform. Saturday was the only time we could sleep in, but I did not take advantage of that luxury.

Only on the weekends the first two months I was there, could I read the Word. I hungered for Living Bread but was not starving. I had enough Word in my spirit man to sustain me. Plus, my Comforter was there cheering me on, speaking life-giving words to me when I felt like giving up. Jesus wants you to know that you can prosper in all circumstances. This is what He is saying to you right now:

Anointed to Prosper

Remember that you have been bought with a price,
purchased with My own blood.
Yes, your character will be tested in a multitude of ways…
But fear not, My precious one…
For I have overcome the world
and you are more than a conqueror in Me,
says the Lord.
Righteousness, peace, and holiness will follow you
all the days of your life.
Never forget you are made in My image
and that your fire pleases Me.
You are anointed to prosper, says your King.

~God, who Reigns ~

God, all at once You turned on a floodlight for me!
You are the revelation-light in my darkness,
and in Your brightness I can see the path ahead.

With You as my strength I can crush an enemy horde,
advancing through every stronghold that stands in front of
me.

What a God You are! Your path for me has been perfect!
All Your promises have proven true.
What a secure shelter for all those who turn to hide them-
selves in You! – Psalm 18:28-30, TPT

After about a month, I started to relax in my routine. I had a better perspective of what was expected of me and I could breathe again. The fear of pushups and bed-making had left me, and I was starting to notice things I had not when I first got there.

God's beautiful creation was all around me. I noticed the birds were singing. I saw deer, wildflowers, and nature. My senses were sharpened and I thought of David in the wilderness when he was fleeing from Saul. On my free time in the evenings, I would go out to one of the picnic tables and read God's Word back to Him. I have never experienced anything like that since. I was reading God's Word to Him like a bedtime story. I inhaled His love and exhaled His Word. He was altogether lovely and I wasted no time in letting Him know it.

PICNIC TABLE DEVOTIONS

O Lord of Heaven's Armies, my King and my God, even the sparrows and swallows are welcome to build a nest among Your altars for the birds to raise their young.

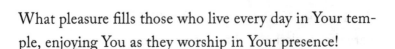

What pleasure fills those who live every day in Your temple, enjoying You as they worship in Your presence!

How enriched are they who find their strength in the Lord; within their hearts are the highways of holiness!

Even when their paths wind through the dark valley of tears, they dig deep to find a pleasant pool where others find only pain.

He gives to them a brook of blessing filled from the rain of an outpouring.
They grow stronger and stronger with every step forward, and the God of all gods will appear before them in Zion.
–Psalm 84:3-7, TPT

WHO ATE MY LUNCH?

In boot camp, there were three phases. Since it was a six-month program, each phase was marked by a different hat color. I had made it through the red and brown hat phases, and now it was blue hat time. You had to pass a series of physical tests to advance to each new hat phase and it was not easy. It would have been impossible to do so when I first got there, but I had gotten in the best shape of my life now after eight weeks of physical training.

I was motivated to become a blue. If you were a blue hat, you were able to go upstairs after dinner to the bedroom and read on your bed, rather than being confined to the living quarters downstairs with all the other plebes. You no longer had to ask permission to use the bathroom, and your chores were not as hard as the other phases. I had dug ditches, chopped and hauled firewood and mowed an entire softball field. As a blue hat, you could do things like crocheting, quilting, and volunteering at the local horse farm doing equine therapy, working with mentally challenged kids. It was hard, but I passed all of my physical tests and finally became a blue hat. Only one more hat phase to complete and then I was done!

I was flabbergasted to find out that no matter how hard I tried, I could not get the hang of crocheting. I would dread recreation class, while all the other girls loved it. They were whipping out blankets for the women's shelters and making scarves and hats for the homeless. Nope, not me. I could not even get a row straight. I would cry myself to sleep at night over crocheting! I was humiliated. Crocheting had eaten my lunch; in the likes of the Mic Jaeger song; "You Can't Always Get What You Want."

So, there I was I was marching towards freedom with only eight weeks to go. Jeff was coming to visit every other week, and I could taste freedom with each step I took. There were only a few more challenges yet to endure, and I would then be home to my husband, my family, my dog, my ministry, my church and my friends.

PLANTED, TILLED AND HARVESTED

Before I knew about boot camp, one day while I was sitting in the medical office in prison, the Lord said; *"Daughter, like Ruth… you will reap a harvest from the threshing floor in a foreign land."* I thought, *What? I'm in a foreign land already!* God was revealing to me mysteries about how His plan for me was likened to these passages in the Bible.

Your threshing shall last till the time of vintage, and the vintage shall last till the time of sowing; you shall eat your bread to the full, and dwell in your land safely.

– Leviticus 26:5, NKJV

They had a *Hollman Bible Dictionary* in the library at boot camp. Every time I opened it up, it kept landing on the harvest seasons of Israel. It took me a month to receive what Holy Spirit was trying to show me and then one day I had an "aha!" moment.

Your threshing shall last till the time of vintage –Ruth went to Bethlehem at the beginning of the Barley Harvest in Israel, which is May. I went to boot camp in May.

And the vintage shall last till the time of sowing – The vintage season in Israel begins in October. I became a blue hat with all of its privileges in October.

Till the time of sowing – The sowing season in Israel is November. I was planted (sowed) back home in November of 2012. I would eat my Living Bread to the full now. I would lie down in my bed at home and dwell in my land safely.

The Lord had the timing of boot camp right down to the seasons of harvest in Israel. That, to me, is mind-blowing!

A WILDERNESS SOLO

Graduation day was soon approaching, but there was one final test awaiting me in boot camp before I could go home. All blue hats needed to do a one-day wilderness solo before graduating. Now, I knew that this would be amazing. I felt completely safe from the

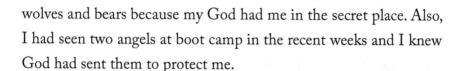

wolves and bears because my God had me in the secret place. Also, I had seen two angels at boot camp in the recent weeks and I knew God had sent them to protect me.

One day while I was prayer-walking in the yard at camp, I looked up. There was a warring sentinel angel standing at attention by the woodpile staring stoically at me. Another time, in the early morning hours, I was lying in bed and saw one walking silently through my barracks. He stopped at my bed and whispered in my ear. He said, "The Lord is your Shepherd, you shall not want." All I can say is that all of the promises in Psalm 23 are true. Beloved, I encourage you to stop reading this book right now and meditate on Psalm 23.

The day finally came for my solo. It was November 6th, 2012. This would be a day I would never forget. My solo campsite happened to be the farthest from the barracks. Something that the Father, no doubt, had arranged. It was the most beautiful November day I can ever remember. The air was so still that you almost could hear the giant snowflakes kiss the ground. It was an unseasonably warm that day as well. My God had fashioned it just for me. It was just Him and I that day. No revelry, no women, and no marching. Absolute stillness… utter bliss.

We had to chop our own wood and make our own fire. Those of you who know me are probably laughing right now at the visual of that. They gave us a brown bag lunch, but if I recall correctly, I had eaten mine by 10:00 am. Mr. Brolin, our recreational therapist, would make rounds and check on us.

We were told that our fires could not be any taller than waist high. Well, God is an all-consuming fire, right? I made my fire and it was so huge, that it was shoulder high. And here I had been worried that I would not be able to get it started! Beloved, God knows your fears and doubts and He is waiting for you to cast your cares upon Him.

> Come to Me, all you who labor and are heavy laden, and I will give you rest. Take My yoke upon you and learn from Me, for I am gentle and lowly in heart, and you will find rest for your souls. For My yoke is easy and My burden is light.
>
> – Matthew 11:28-30, NKJV

Here is what your King says to you at this moment:

Branded by the Lord

My Mishkan....[13]

Cast all your care upon Me.

Fear not My child,

for you are destined for greatness!

I sear you with the fire of My brand.

You are untouchable.

You are crisp, clean, beautiful and white.

Your Lord and King receives you and all your requests.

~Messiah, King of Kings ~

---

13 The Tabernacle in Hebrew = Mishkan "Residence" or "dwelling place" the portable earthly dwelling place for the Shekinah

SUPERNATURALLY SWEETENED

Finally, the day arrived. I was graduating from boot camp! Jeff was coming to take me home. I had run my wilderness race, completed my course. My forty-month sentence had ended up being fourteen months. I knew My King was well pleased with me, and it was well with my soul.

After the ceremony, Jeff surprised me. As soon as I climbed into his truck, he took my wedding ring out of his pocket and slipped it back on my finger. *What?* It looked different. He had doubled the size of my diamond! I wept. It had more meaning to me than you can imagine. It was so prophetic, as a diamond is composed of pure carbon. In order for carbon to crystallize in the form of diamond, *tremendous temperatures and pressures are required.*

My precious husband had also brought with him the elements for us to have Holy Communion together. We took communion right then and there in his truck and thanked the Lord for His blood covenant. I shed tears as I write this part. My husband is the greatest treasure that the Father has ever given me after Jesus. There are no English words that can describe the gratitude I have for him. Thank you, Father. No matter what you are going through right now, As He delivered me, He will deliver you!

On the drive home, I looked back at my time in the wilderness. I saw that the Lord not only delivered me from all my afflictions, He also kept me from walking into any snares / traps that the devil had set for me. See His promise to do that for you as well:

Released from the Snare of the Fowler

You are released / delivered from the snare of the fowler.

You have walked through the fire and not gotten scorched.

It is My pleasure to give you My kingdom.

You are intricately and curiously wrought.

My glory shall shine through you.

~Your Lord has spoken~

When you pass through the waters, I will be with you; and through the rivers, they shall not overflow you. When you walk through the fire, you shall not be burned, nor shall the flame scorch you. – Isaiah 43:2, NKJV

PART THREE
To the Table ...

So [MB] changed from her prison garments,

and she ate bread regularly

before the King all the days of her life.

And as for her provisions,

there was a regular ration given her by the King,

a portion for each day until the day of her death,

all the days of her life.

Jeremiah 52:33-34, NKJV (personalized)

Chapter 9

BACK TO LIFE...
BACK TO REALITY

I waited and waited and waited some more,
patiently, knowing God would come through for me.
Then, at last, He bent down and listened to my cry.
He stooped down to lift me out of danger
from the desolate pit I was in,
out of the muddy mess I had fallen into.
Now He's lifted me up into a firm, secure place
and steadied me while I walk along His ascending path.
A new song for a new day rises up in me
every time I think about how He breaks through for me!
Ecstatic praise pours out of my mouth
until everyone hears how God has set me free.
Many will see His miracles;
they'll stand in awe of God and fall in love with Him!

– Psalm 40:1-3, TPT –

FORWARD MARCH

Once I got back home, I felt like the expression, "Back in the saddle again," except everything was sweeter now. I wept with gratitude on a regular basis. I repented for taking the little things in life from my past for granted. I had come out of the fiery furnace without the smell of smoke, because my Redeemer King had been in there with me the entire time.

Who is this one? Look at her now!
She arises out of her desert, clinging to her Beloved.
– Song of Solomon 8:5, TPT

One day shortly after I came home, the Lord spoke to me and said:

"Daughter, I allowed this trial not because of unrighteousness (crimes committed in my past) but "because" of your righteousness.

"This trial was to establish in you a deeper insight into your relationship with Me. I wanted to give you a greater understanding of the sincerity of your faith. I did not allow this trial to see if you'd fail, but rather to strengthen and to reveal to you My confidence in your perseverance and integrity."

Beloved friend of God… If you are in the midst of adverse circumstances right now, know that your Redeemer lives and He WILL bring you through to the other side!

He speaks this over you:

My child,

Get ready to be plunged into the deep.

For I will pull you into the depths of My ocean.

The ocean of love, grace and mercy.

Mysteries, power and provision are yours for the taking.

I am decorating you as a war hero.

~Crucified Lamb of God~

It was almost surreal to be back home again after fourteen months. I was land-locked to the house most of the time for the next six months due to what was called ISR: Intensive Supervised Release. I had to be accounted for every minute of my day. If I was "spot-checked" and not where I was supposed to be, I could be sent back to prison at a moment's notice.

Probation officers would come to our house in the middle of the night for random urine tests. I even had to get permission to attend church. They also monitored drive-time to and from where I was going. There were many times when I was caught in traffic and found myself praying in tongues. But then I would remember that God had brought me this far. Nothing would happen to change that, especially with circumstances that were out of my control.

I settled back into my old routine quickly. I was relieved that my wilderness test was behind me, but I was wrong. I still had the last piece of the puzzle to walk out. Walking back into my church was a little daunting. Hardly anyone knew that I had been in a three-year criminal courts process, let alone that I had even been charged with a financial crime. Only my family and inner-circle friends had journeyed down this road with me. All of a sudden one day, people noticed that I was gone. People came to Jeff in droves asking him where I was, and he had the grim task of telling them that I was in prison.

This was where the rubber met the road for us. It was shocking to see who our true friends were. Some of the most obvious friends we thought we had, never came to see me or even send me a card in prison. They also never even checked on Jeff. It was astounding to me. Yet, there were people that barely knew me who wrote to me on a regular basis. I will never forget that, and to them I am truly grateful.

To top it off, the Lord told me to *ZIP MY LIP* about why He had allowed me to go to prison. I had to hold my head up high, walk into church and not say a peep. Most people did not know my crimes were old and had been committed before I was sober or knew Jesus. Most certainly, some assumed I had recently committed a felony and was sent to prison. In any event, the big moment came, and I walked in. I was astounded at the love and hugs of joy I received from people. My pastor even came over and welcomed me back. Once again, I had to repent for allowing the enemy of my soul to build a case against others in my mind.

Love bears up under anything and everything that comes is ever ready to believe the best of every person, its hopes are fadeless under all circumstances, and it endures everything [without weakening]. – 1 Corinthians 13:7, AMPC

This last piece of this test reminded me that there is no shame for those that are in Christ Jesus. (Romans 8:1)

THE DAWN OF A NEW ERA

Eight weeks after I returned home, I had something happen that shook me to my core. My spiritual mom, Loni, died abruptly from a brain aneurysm. Jeff and I were driving on the way to church when we got the call. I was in shock. WHAT? *I have only been home, Lord, for eight weeks and now another loss?* I almost couldn't take it. Upon hearing the news that Loni was in the hospital, our mutual friend, Jon, heard the following as he was going up in the elevator to see her. It sounded like a police scanner. He heard; "411 in progress." It was not until years later that I received the revelation of what this meant. In spite of my training by Holy Spirit in prison, I found myself still "depending" on Loni at times, to find out what the Lord was saying. *411 in progress* was the making of a prophet. Ephesians 4:11 says;

And He Himself gave some to be apostles, some prophets, some evangelists, and some pastors and teachers.

Let me be perfectly clear. God was not the author of Loni's death. However, even though her home-going was shocking and painful to so many of us, in my case, He used her home-going in a Romans 8:28 fashion:

And we know that all things work together for good to those who love God, to those who are the called according to His purpose.

ON MY OWN AGAIN

In the *natural*, I was on my own again. I had been alone in prison, and now with no spiritual mom there to guide me, I felt lost. I had Holy Spirit, of course, but I am referring to losing a spiritual mentor's fellowship and wisdom. I had Jeff, but there are shoes that only a spiritual mom can fill. I encourage you, ladies, to ask someone you admire in the faith to be your spiritual mother, and for you men, a spiritual father.

I want to thank Twila for stepping in and carrying the baton that Loni passed on to her. In many ways, Twila has done more than fill Loni's shoes. She has become a great friend. She was my boss for seven years, and now that she's retired, we continue on in a mother-daughter relationship. I love you so much, Twila!

Speaking of spiritual motherhood, God surprised me again. At Loni's home-going celebration, two people prophesied that I would take on the mantel (assignment) of spiritual motherhood. It was the last thing on my mind at the time, but God knew better. He has blessed me with spiritual daughters that I've had the pleasure to mentor. I have watched them grow and prosper in the kingdom and it has been amazing to watch. More on that later.

A TRIP TO THE BROOK CHERITH

Several months later, I was lying in bed one night and the Lord gave me a vision. It was as though I left my body and was looking down at Jeff and me sleeping. All of a sudden, a raven flew in and set itself down between us. The next morning, Holy Spirit led me to 1 Kings 17:2-5, NKJV.

> Then the word of the Lord came to him, saying, "Get away from here and turn eastward, and hide by the Brook Cherith, which flows into the Jordan. And it will be that you shall drink from the brook, and I have commanded the ravens to feed you there." So he went and did according to the word of the Lord, for he went and stayed by the Brook Cherith, which flows into the Jordan. The ravens brought him bread and meat in the morning, and bread and meat in the evening; and he drank from the brook.

The Lord was bringing us into a new season of His nourishment. I knew that the Brook Cherith represented Living Water, and that the bread and the meat represented the Bread of Life and the meat of the Word. What an amazing time in my life. I was saturated in the Word and my appetite for it was insatiable.

> And Jesus said to them, "I am the Bread of Life. He who comes to Me shall never hunger, and he who believes in Me shall never thirst." – John 6:35, NKJV

Friend of God, the Lord is calling you to go deeper into the Word. Jesus IS the Word, and He is beckoning you to get to know Him on a deeper level of intimacy.

Deep Cries unto Deep

Make yourself available to the deeper things of God.

Ratchet up your faith for divinely inspired revelation.

Get ready to be launched deeper into intimacy with Me.

Keep your thought life pure, clean, and holy

by meditating in My word.

Deep cries unto deep, My child.

~*Bread of Life*~

GOD'S IN NO HURRY

So here I was, waiting on the Lord to "Send me!" I was ready, willing and able to be about my Father's business again, now that I was on the outside and fully released from restrictions. But all He said to me was, "Stay tuned for further instructions."

He told me that there was "fine-tuning" yet to be done, and that I needed to be patient. For those of you who have "waited on the Lord," you know how difficult that can be.

I knew the following scripture well after coming home, and I was ready to serve my Lord in a greater measure. Prison had broken off of me the fear of man and man could no longer do anything to me.

To grant us that we, being delivered from the hand of our enemies, might serve Him without fear. –Luke 1:74, NKJV

I felt like a horse at the starting gate of a race, waiting to be released to run. Like it is written in Hebrews 12:1; I felt like I had thrown off all weights that encumbered me in prison/boot camp and was ready to go, but God's timing is always better than ours.

Therefore, we also, since we are surrounded by so great a cloud of witnesses, let us lay aside every weight, and the sin which so easily ensnares us, and let us run with endurance the race that is set before us – Hebrews 12:1, NKJV

Are you in a season of waiting on the Lord, right now? I hope the word on the following page encourages you.

Let Patience Have its Perfect Work

Let patience have its perfect work, Ma Petite Maison.[14]

You have been carefully chosen; not randomly selected.

You've walked with Me through the fire.

Watch Me go to war on your behalf...

For no weapon forged against you will prosper.

Those who come against you, come against Me.

For I will raise you up to the likes the world has never seen before...

Because you have walked not in the counsel of the ungodly.

You are a change agent in My Temple, and I've anointed you

with great forbearance and illumination.

Realms of fire and glory...

an awakening of the Spirit surrounds you.

Matchless authority poured out from the windows of Heaven

upon you.

~Messiah King~

---

14 (My Little Dwelling; in French)

Chapter 10

AND SO, WE BEGIN...

*Now the Lord came and stood and called as at other
times, "Samuel! Samuel!" And Samuel answered,
"Speak, for Your servant hears."*

– 1 Samuel 3:10, NKJV –

SPEAK LORD,
FOR YOUR SERVANT IS LISTENING

*W*e know from the account in 1 Samuel, that Samuel not only heard the voice of the Lord, but he *requested* it. When I go into my prayer closet in the morning, I say what Samuel said. Before I go to bed at night, I also decree;

I sleep but my heart is awake…it's the voice of my Beloved.
– Song of Solomon 5:2, NKJV

Friend of God… He has so much He wants to share with you! This is one of the main reasons I wrote this book. These throne-room words He has spoken to me, are for YOU! They contain the "Heartbeat of Heaven," and He wants to share His heart with you. I also want to encourage you to ask Him to speak to you directly, and then get in a quiet place. Most certainly you will hear His voice. He will also speak to you through His Word. The more you read the Word, the more you will be sensitive to the things of the Spirit. I believe that not only will you hear His voice through the throne-room words in this book, but also in your devotional time in an increased measure. Hear His voice as He speaks to you now.

Beautiful in God's Sight

My precious child… you have captivated My heart!

I have so much to give you, so much to share with you,

so much to pour out on you!

Listen to Me! You are fearless and bold!

Follow the yellow brick road to charity (love).

Know that my Love towards you abounds to every good work.

Seek Me, love Me, find Me, breathe Me, pursue Me,

and ravish Me with your love!

Time is on your side.

~Your Master Decrees This.~

GOD SPEAKS "AFTER" THE FIRE

It says in 1 Kings 19:12:

And after the earthquake a fire, but the Lord was not in the fire; and **after the fire**, a still small voice.

Right before the Lord speaks to me, I get "fire." I literally feel His fiery presence on my body. The Bible says, "For our God is a consuming fire" (Hebrews 12:29; NKJV).

Fire is a wonderful picture of the work of the Holy Spirit. The Spirit is like a fire in at least three ways: He brings God's presence, God's passion, and God's purity. The Holy Spirit is the presence of God as He indwells the heart of the believer. Even if you do not physically feel His fiery presence, know that it is there. The following word was spoken to me for you, His beautiful bride!

Fiery Stones

My Royal Chariot awaits you,

My dearest darling.

Your ball gown is of fiery stones.

We will dance the night away,

and catch a sunrise.

~*Your Royal Bridegroom~*

THE BIRTH OF A BINDER

I can't put my finger on the exact date, but one day in 2013, I began to use technology to record everything the Lord said. I used to have to journal everything He said, because I had no electronic devices in prison. My hand used to cramp up because I could not write fast enough. Thank you, Holy Spirit, for giving mankind the technology for electronics!

Now, when I get the fire anointing, I grab my phone and speak *exactly* what He says to me. As I speak, it types it out in my phone, I then email it to myself, find an image to insert into the document, and print it off. Eventually, I got the idea to put these words in 3-ring binders. At this moment in time, I have thirteen 3-ring binders that contain over 700 beautiful throne-room words. Some of them are in this book. Others have been for certain individuals personally. (You know who you are). In any event, I hold these as sacred treasures. Until writing this book, I stewarded them in my heart and gave them to others as the Lord directed.

One day in May 2017, the Lord orchestrated a divine appointment with Rhonda Kitabjian, President of Royal Business Consulting, whom I only knew casually, from "Women in Ministry Network." On a phone call with Rhonda (that originated from a Facebook post I had made), she was instructed by Holy Spirit, through a word-of-knowledge, that it was time for me to take these "binder words" out from under a lampshade, and publish them for all the world to see. This was the beginning of *Summoned out of Darkness.* Thank you, Rhonda, for being obedient to the call to be the spiritual midwife for this book!

THE RAIN IN SPAIN

I take painstaking care to only speak what He speaks. After all, I paid a very high price to learn the danger of misapplying a prophetic word. You may remember the movie; "My Fair Lady." If you do, the following will make sense to you. If I start to detour even slightly from what He has said, (because I did not transcribe it with

100% accuracy), He says; *Daughter! The rain in Spain falls mainly on the plain!* I love His sense of humor!

Occasionally, Holy Spirit pours oil on my head as He speaks. I equate this experience to when Jesus says in the Word; *"Verily, Verily I say unto you."*

And you shall make of these a holy anointing oil, a perfume compounded after the art of the perfumer; it shall be a sacred anointing oil. –Exodus 30:25, AMPC

Beloved, these words have your name on them. I am honored to bring forth His life-giving words to you through this book. He is calling for you to come up higher. Here is what He is saying to you right now:

~*Rainbows of Light*~

My Raiment…

Exquisite Raiment showers you My precious one.

Glistening, dancing and catching…

shining rays from My presence.

Rainbows of light from Heaven above…

beckoning you to come up higher into the realms of Me.

Feast on revelation poured out through this Light.

Catapulted into your destiny, you shall go.

Spirit of the Living God

A FISH OUT OF WATER

Have you ever felt like a fish out of water, or a square peg trying to fit into a round hole? That is how I felt as I waited for the next move of God in my life. What I realize now is that God was preparing me with content for this book. Throne-room words started coming in rapid succession. He was speaking to me non-stop, and I didn't want to miss a thing! I was in awe of My Lord. It was utterly mind-blowing to me that the God who created the universe would use someone like me to bring His life-giving words to you, the reader.

The reason I felt like a fish out of water was that I did not know initially what to do with it all. He kept speaking, and I kept printing off these words and putting them into binders. Many times, we so often try to get ahead of Him, but only He knows the end from the beginning. Often times, there are years of preparation for a calling. For example, look at King David. He was called out to be King of Israel at a young age, when he was only a shepherd boy.

I heard Pastor Mac say one time in church that you don't give car keys to a 3-year-old, even though you know he will drive some-day. That is way of the Lord. He lovingly prepares us in our callings every step of the way. He says that His word is a lamp unto our feet and a light unto our path (Psalm 119:105, KJV). Isn't that amazing? We have a book of life to guide us. It is said that the acronym for the Bible is "Basic Instructions Before Leaving Earth." Waiting on the Lord is not always easy, but know that He is working on your behalf, and His timing is always perfect.

DELUSIONS OF GRANDEUR

During these waiting years, I often imagined that I would be on the world stage, speaking from pulpits saying, "Thus says the Lord." It often led to disappointment as my big moment never came, but that has since changed. I had no idea at that time that God would raise me up to minister to His children prophetically through this book, television, radio and through social media.

His plan for our lives is always better than anything we could ever possibly imagine

I have come to see that many people want the calling, but are unwilling to *pay the price* to walk in it. A great anointing always demands a great price.

Jesus said; "For many are called, but few are chosen."
—Matthew 22:14, NKJV

For unto whosoever much is given, of him shall much be required. – Luke 12:48, KJV

Those who are willing to pay the price will carry the anointing. Because of its costliness, they must put their complete trust and confidence in God. Oftentimes, it is not the stress of attaining the achievement, but simply the inability to endure and trust God to bring to pass that which He has promised. Are you willing to pay the price, beloved? "Humble yourselves, therefore, under the mighty hand of God so that at the proper time He may exalt you" (1 Peter 5:6). Be willing beloved to pay the price, for it will surely come to pass. Hear what He is saying to you now. This is His promise to those who humble themselves:

Exalted Before Royalty

For I will exalt thee before kings, queens, and noblemen.

For you have sought after Me with your whole heart

and not put the cart before the horse.

Now it is My turn to give you praise!

You are a fragrant offering to Me, My child.

Walk out your calling with boldness and authority

for new assignments are forthcoming.

Tell of Me in Judea and Samaria

and to all the ends of the earth.

Speak life to the dry bones in people's lives.

For I have reared you up in the way you should go,

and knowledge and wisdom are in your countenance.

Together, we shall fight the good fight of faith!

~King Jesus~

NEW SPECIES OF PROPHET

On July 3rd, 2015, the Lord said; "You are My new species of prophet." I got it. He was using me to go to individuals in a very unique way. As these words in my binders accumulated, He would tell me who to make binders for, and I was obedient to do so. If you have a binder from me, then you know this. Now, of course, He has

released me to give you the reader, your very own set of throne-room words throughout this book. He told me that my binders contained the "Heartbeat of Heaven." It was during that season that I started hearing the lyrics to the song from The Herman's Hermits:

Every time I see you looking' my way,
baby, baby, can't you hear my heartbeat?
In the car or walking down the highway baby, baby,
can't you hear my heartbeat? [15]

And so, the *Heartbeat of Heaven* goes on and on and on.

---

15 "Can't You Hear My Heartbeat?"; Lyrics by John Carter and Ken Louis

Chapter 11

THE BIRTHING
OF A LIONESS

And Mary sang this song:

"My soul is ecstatic, overflowing with praises to God!

My spirit bursts with joy over my life-giving God.

For He set His tender gaze upon me,

His lowly servant girl.

And from here on, everyone will know

that I have been favored and blessed.

The Mighty One has worked a mighty miracle for me;

Holy is His name!

Mercy kisses all His godly lovers,

from one generation to the next.

– Song of Mary/ Luke 1:46-50, TPT –

THE WOMB PHASE

I mentioned in an earlier chapter that in May, 2011, I had a vision of a fetus floating around my bedroom, that I knew to be my spiritual baby. Also, while lying in bed in prison in November, 2011, my baby had leapt in my womb. It was just like John the Baptist did in Elizabeth's womb. God had impregnated me with something I was going to give birth to, and I was ready! This baby was conceived in spirit, love and in truth. Halleluiah!

> Shall I bring to the time of birth, and not cause delivery?" says the Lord "Shall I who cause delivery shut up the womb?" says your God. – Isaiah 66:8, , NKJV

Are you pregnant with something God is going to birth in you? Does it feel impossible or that you've been waiting forever? Take note of what Hebrews 11:11 says about Sarah, whom God had promised a child. Sarah gave birth long after her child-bearing years, because she BELIEVED God, who had promised it to her.

> By faith, Sarah herself also received strength to conceive seed, and she bore a child when she was past the age because she judged Him faithful who had promised.
> – Hebrews 11:11, NKJV

The Lord says to you right now:

Lord, I Will Wait

My child…

You are sanctified, consecrated, anointed, rectified,

and purified to do kingdom business.

As John was in the wilderness;

so are you in this season of waiting.

Hang on, My child, you're almost there.

You and your destiny were procreated by Me

before the foundation of the earth.

I will send you forth to accomplish My kingdom purposes.

For you will be glorified through Me,

My Little Dwelling, and all that I show you.

Others have gotten ahead of Me

and have not waited for My perfect timing,

and they will self-destruct in their haste.

But not you, My child,

you have patiently endured the preparatory season

that I commissioned you to go through.

Everything I do is pre-planned out.

You're alive in the fiery stones of My Heart.

~Resurrected King~

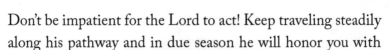
Don't be impatient for the Lord to act! Keep traveling steadily along his pathway and in due season he will honor you with every blessing. –Psalm 37:34, TLB

Can a baby eat meat? The answer is yes! While you are going through your development phase, read as much "meat" of the Word as you can. It is crucially important to do so, as faith comes by hearing and hearing the Word of God. Faith is so important to help birth what you are carrying.

In the natural, the baby is nourished by the food the mother eats. So, eat the meat of the word as much as you can, so what you birth, will be grounded in the word.

Take your prenatal vitamins too – anything that nourishes you as you go through this process, like praise and worship. Also, surround yourself with like-minded friends and believers that encourage you through this process. Take Mary and Elizabeth for example:

And Mary remained with her (Elizabeth) about three months, and returned to her house. – Luke 1:56, NKJV

There are times when you may feel your baby kicking and screaming to get out. That is normal. It is important to know that patience is a fruit of the Spirit given to you by Holy Spirit. Even if you are not aware of it, the Father is always working behind the scenes with ministering angels, to put things in order for you to walk into your destiny!

Sometimes there are people in our lives that either need to come in or go. God has a way of removing toxic relationships in our lives that can hinder us and slow us down. He also arranges people to come into our lives that are needed for our purpose to be fulfilled.

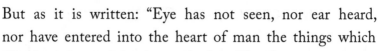

But as it is written: "Eye has not seen, nor ear heard, nor have entered into the heart of man the things which God has prepared for those who love Him."

–1 Corinthians 2:9, NKJV

Maybe your calling is to go to a particular people group. God might have to prepare your heart and their hearts as well, so they are ready to receive what it is you are carrying. God has packed your luggage with everything you need to carry out His perfect will for your life. Keep pressing into Him, faithful one, for He will surely bring it to pass. If we get ahead of God, we can either miscarry our spiritual baby or birth an Ishmael. Here is His promise to you as you go through the birthing process:

A Handbreadth Away

Recompense awaits you, My child.
You are kissing the feet of My Son
who bled for you when you worship.
Keep still… for the night season beckons you.
Kindred spirits we are.
Your fulfilled destiny is a mere handbreadth away.

~Messiah King; The One who calls you~

SUPERNATURAL CHILDBIRTH

The Lord has a multitude of ways to keep us excited along the way. Mine is a very unique story.

One day He said to me, "*I am going to induce labor for you to give birth. I will be your midwife.*"

Here is the timeline of my pregnancy and supernatural birth:

May, 2011 / Vision of fetus floating in my bedroom

November 2011 / My baby leapt in my womb

May 22nd, 2014 / I was alone in the restroom at the doctor's office. There were three empty stalls when I entered the bathroom. As I entered my stall, and before I could even close the stall door, I heard a loud door slam and I heard the words "I AM GABRIEL!"

Wow. How do you explain that one? You can't. The Lord wanted me to know that the birth was coming soon because Gabriel was the messenger angel.

July 29th, 2014 / I asked the Lord, "*When am I giving birth to my baby?*" I then immediately heard Holy Spirit say, "*Twas the Night before Christmas*" (a mystery I will reveal soon). Then He spoke and said:

"*Surround yourself in My Word. I will guide you where to navigate through it.*

"*Do not hurry this process. There are mysteries that I will reveal to you that will be necessary for you to uncover before you give birth. It is with great fear and trepidation that the enemy fears this birthing of a Queen. A royal diadem (Tiara) I will place on your head.*"

After this, I noticed a female duck resting in the back yard for quite some time. He said, *"Her name is Natasha, and upon My command, she flew into your yard. Observe how she rests."* So, I looked up the definition of the name Natasha, and it means; *"A birthday on or born near Christmas."* My spiritual mom Loni had prophesied that the Lord was going to give me a special gift on Christmas. WOW. I was ready to give birth, and the anticipation was exciting!

Born of the Feast of Trumpets

As Christians, the designated date chosen to celebrate the birth of Jesus is December 25th. Did you know that, according to many scholars, Jesus was actually born in September? The Apostle John may have seen importance in these extraordinary occurrences when he symbolically showed that Jesus was born at the New Moon of Tishri, on the Day of Trumpets (See Revelation 12:1–3). Remember that the Lord told me that my baby would be born *Twas the Night Before Christmas?* He had also said *Natasha* to me, which means, "To be born on or *near* Christmas. I had a vision of my baby being born on September 23rd, 2014. The Feast of Trumpets in 2014 (Christ's birthday) was September 25th. Amazing God!

The Vision of My Birth to Scheherazade

The Birthing of a Queen (September 23, 2014)

Last night I gave birth.
I had a vision in the night of me in a birthing room.
My head was covered with a surgical cap.
I was in a great bright white light.

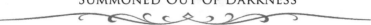
My baby came out and it was HUGE.

It turned/changed into me as it came out.

The Lord named my baby Scheherazade; meaning…

"She… whose realm or dominion is free"

"Lion Born" and "World-Freer"

The Lord told me that the enemy fears this birthing of a queen.

I heard the "Halleluiah Chorus" upon waking.

I could not make up the above if you paid me a million dollars. My point is that the Lord has BIG plans for your life. He will move heaven and earth to bring them to pass. All you need to be is willing and obedient to His plans and purposes for your life.

MARRIED TO THE LION OF JUDAH

He named my baby Scheherazade, which means *"lion-born/ world-freer."* I was coming fully into who God had called me to be and my destiny was being birthed in this new season.

Scheherazade wrote this book. He called me to publish beautiful throne-room words to inspire you and bring you into a greater relationship with the Father. In the last section of this book, "The Heartbeat of Heaven; Love Declarations from the Father's Heart," you will encounter His love for you in full measure.

It is my sincerest hope and prayer, that as you read the pages of this book, you will be inspired to pursue a greater measure of intimacy with Jesus.

We are lionesses married to the Lion of the Tribe of Judah. In the natural, lionesses "hunt" for the male. Are you hunting for people to show the love of the Father to? Are you hunting for souls to save? Jesus, the Lion of the Tribe of Judah, wants you to hunt for Him. The Lord says to you right now, *"I am issuing you a hunting license!"*

Chapter 12

FREE TO MOVE ABOUT THE CABIN

The Captain (Jesus) has turned off the fasten seatbelt sign.
You are free to move about the cabin.

THE OATH OF OFFICE

The Lord has called Me from the womb; from the matrix of my mother He has made mention of my name. And He has made My mouth like a sharp sword; In the shadow of His hand He has hidden Me, and made me a polished shaft; In His quiver He has hidden me. – Isaiah 49:1-2, NKJV

I love that scripture. The Lord *does* hide us until the appropriate time comes for Him to commission us into our callings. It is in that hiddenness, where He plows deep into the soil of our hearts. He fertilizes what needs to be grown and pulls out any weeds that might hinder us in our destiny. There is always a preparatory season before we walk out our true destiny.

Lord, I have chosen You alone as my inheritance. You are my prize, my pleasure, and my portion. I leave my destiny and its timing in Your hands. –Psalm 16:5, TPT

As we learn to trust Him more and more... we will boldly walk out our callings with blessed assurance. Beloved one, He has placed in you all of the authority, talents, and gifts you will need in order to fulfill your destiny when it is your appointed time. With Him guiding you along the way, you can accomplish all that He has ordained you to do. Are you waiting to move about the cabin? Sometimes all we need is a nudge from our co-pilot, Holy Spirit.

On June 29th, 2014 I was lying in bed trying to fall asleep. All of a sudden, I felt the holy presence of the Lord come into my bedroom. I held my breath as I felt Him coming closer and closer. I dared not even open my eyes as the fear of the Lord hit me in full force. All of a sudden, I felt Him pour oil over my head. As it ran down the sides of my face, He spoke:

"Arise and thresh, oh beautiful daughter, and receive your commission. For I have called you to the ends of the earth for My glory. I give you the authority to trample on serpents and scorpions. You will consecrate what you thresh to Me... souls that have been stolen by the evil one.

"I give you all power and authority from the throne room to do this most holy assignment. You will hear a voice that says; 'This is the way... walk in it!' I, The Lord, have spoken."

Then He said,

"Repeat after Me: 'I solemnly swear that I will faithfully execute the Office of Prophet to the best of my ability... so help me God.'"

So, I did!

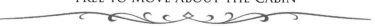

After I took the oath of office, I came to know a boldness I had never known before. God knows when we are ready! Are you ready? Ask the Lord for more patience if you have not been released yet, and He will give it to you. Sometimes when we are commissioned, there is fear that we will make a mistake.

Beloved, as long as you have a willing and obedient heart, and are in constant communication and submission to Him, there is no reason to allow the fear of making mistakes paralyze you and keep you from fulfilling what you have been called to do. The teacher is always there to guide you. He will always move heaven and earth on your behalf. He says to you right now...

Knighted by the King

Are you ready to be shot like a cannon into your destiny?
Forward march!
A seasoned veteran you are...
battle tested, anointed and fearless to go into battle.
Pick up your sword and fight
for the right to speak the oracles of God!
I will orchestrate your steps to put you into position.
Character assassination will come,
but "Blessed are the persecuted for righteousness sake,
for theirs is the kingdom of God" (Matthew 5:10).
Now go present yourself to the King
so He can knight you for battle.

~Spirit of the Living God~

A FRAGRANT OFFERING

The Word says that we are a fragrant offering unto the Lord.

We have become the unmistakable aroma of the victory of the Anointed One to God - a perfume of life to those being saved and the odor of death to those who are perishing.

– 2 Corinthians 2:15, TPT

I love how the Word can even take us deeper into this. The following was taken from the teaching notes in my *Revival Study Bible*.[16]

Praise, worship, and prayer are never separated biblically. The recipe Moses used for the holy incense describes a perfect balance of certain characteristics needed in praise, worship, and prayer. Each spice represents one of these qualities. An overemphasis of any one of these qualities brings imbalance and is unacceptable to God.

And the Lord said to Moses: "Take sweet spices, stacte and onycha and galbanum, and pure frankincense with these sweet spices; there shall be equal amounts of each. You shall make of these an incense, a compound according to the art of the perfumer, salted, pure, and holy." –Exodus 30:34-35, NKJV

Stacte = Speaking words in prophetic inspiration.

Onycha = A lion's roar. Indicating that praise, worship, and prayer need to be lionlike and bold.

---

16 *Revival Study Bible;* Tamara Winslow and Steve Hill, General Editors; Armour Publishing

Galbanum = A fatty substance used as a medicine to stop spasms; represents self-control and giving the best to God.

Frankincense = Represents holiness.

Salt = An earthy and gaseous combination; it is added and symbolizes heaven and earth in agreement.

That is so cool. My WIMN leader, Michelle Burkett, said to me one time, "*God leaves no stitch undone.*" This is what He says to you right now:

It's Time

You think you've seen My best?
Get ready for an outpouring that will take your breath away!
You are so beautiful to Me, you know.
The time has come to walk in the fullness
of what I have called you to do.
For I have chosen you for a task that will awaken
the breath of My Spirit within you.
Faithfully endure what comes your way.
Your destiny is sacred!
You are a fragrant offering to Me,
so, remember that you please Me.

~Papa God~

The Reluctant Intercessor

I read somewhere that not all intercessors are prophets but that all prophets are intercessors. Yikes, really? "But God, I want to be the one who is out and about prophesying over people and making them happy! Why do I have to be on my knees in my prayer closet all the time?" The thought of that wasn't exactly a desire of mine. But God! It was God's mandate for me to go deeper into His heart and he wishes that for you too! He wants to open up to us revelation and secrets that are hidden for us to find. Did you know that God's desires become our desires? Why? Because He puts them there.

> Delight yourself also in the Lord, and He shall give you the desires of your heart. Commit your way to the Lord, trust also in Him, and He shall bring it to pass. –Psalm 37:4-5, NKJV

Isn't that so awesome? HE gives us the desires of our heart. In other words, His desires become our desires. So now, here I am today, as an intercessor on my knees at 4:00 AM every morning. Whatever it is He has called you to do, He will give you the desire to do so. His desire then becomes your desire. All He needs is a heart that is turned towards Him. Are you all in?

Praying to Him and worshipping Him when we get up in the morning is the best way to start the day. When we give the Lord our first-fruits of the day, things will be well with our souls. If I don't start my day with the Lord, then I suffer during the day with little things, because I didn't invite Him into my day. Prayer is simply

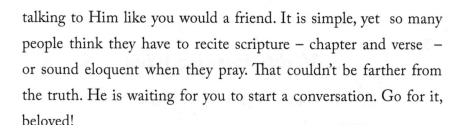
talking to Him like you would a friend. It is simple, yet so many people think they have to recite scripture – chapter and verse – or sound eloquent when they pray. That couldn't be farther from the truth. He is waiting for you to start a conversation. Go for it, beloved!

THERE IS WAINSCOTING IN THE TEMPLE

One day, the Lord said to me the word, "Wainscoting." My immediate reaction was like, *huh*? Wainscoting is wooden paneling that lines the lower part of the walls of a room. Then He led me to Ezekiel 41:16 where Ezekiel is shown God's temple design.

And the galleries all around their 3 stories opposite the threshold, were paneled with wood from the ground to the windows. – Ezekiel 41:16, NKJV

The wainscoting is about being in the heavenly temple of the Most-High God. The threshold is the gateway into the Holy of Holies, the three stories represent the Holy Trinity, the wood paneling is the cross, and the windows are our spiritual eyes. When we pray on our knees (the ground), we can look up with our spiritual eyes (the windows) and receive revelation from the Lord. We have blessed assurance that He hears our prayers. Amazing!

When we see through the eyes of the cross, we can expect the breakthrough He promises in the following...

A Mighty Rushing Wind

There is a breakthrough coming in the spirit realm!
A mighty rushing wind that will take you by surprise.
You will cry out for mercy and you will rejoice with
thanksgiving...
When this glory has risen upon you!
This type of glory you've never experienced before.
It is matchless and anointed...
It's glory beyond your ability
to understand with your natural mind.
Get ready to receive, My mighty warrior!
Your King beckons you to come up higher!
Instrumental to your receiving
is the "wainscoting" in the temple.

~Your Crucified King~

QUEEN MOTHER

She rises also while it is still night and gives food to her household, and portions to her maidens. – Proverbs 31:15, NKJV

Speaking of praying for others.... I mentioned that after my spiritual mom Loni died, I was given the assignment by the Lord to be a spiritual mom to others. At the time, I had no idea what I was doing. He kept bringing women into my life to edify and encourage

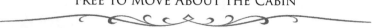

in the Word. As He did, I applied my knowledge of the Word to help these precious women apply spiritual truths to their daily lives. The more I did, the more women He brought me.

"Sing, barren woman, who has never had a baby. Fill the air with song, you who've never experienced childbirth! You're ending up with far more children than all those childbearing women." God says so! "Clear lots of ground for your tents! Make your tents large. Spread out! Think big! Use plenty of rope, drive the tent pegs deep. You're going to need lots of elbow room for your growing family."

– Isaiah 54:1, MSG

We are all called to disciple nations, and that includes spiritual children. Friend of God, when you feel ready, pray that He bring you sons and daughters to help grow in the Word. You have, deposited inside of you, everything you need. You don't have to have a degree in theology either. All you need is a willing heart that desires to minister to others. The following is not only a promise for biological children, but to your spiritual children as well:

All your children shall be taught by the Lord, and great shall be the peace of your children. – Isaiah 54:13, NKJV

I hear the Lord saying to you right now as I type this... *Rejoice in your portion!* Your portion is more than enough to equip others by coming alongside of them.

Chapter 13

HARNESSED TO THE CHARIOT OF THE KING

Is this the little girl I carried? Is this the little boy at play?

I don't remember growing older, when, did, they?

When did she get to be a beauty?

When did he grow to be so tall?

Wasn't it yesterday when they, were, small?

Sunrise, sunset, sunrise, sunset, swiftly flow the days

Seedlings turn overnight to sunflower,

blossoming even as we gaze.[17]

THE DAPPLED HORSE

One of my first visions after getting called to the office of prophet was of a beautiful dappled horse. It appeared to me in our family room in all its splendor. At the time, I did not understand the vision until I received the scripture attached to that vision.

17 "Sunrise Sunset"; From the "Musical Fiddler on the Roof"; Songwriters; Jerry Bock & Sheldon Harnick Sung by Anthony Hewley & Linda Hibberd

My dearest one... let Me tell you how I see you. You are so thrilling to me. To gaze upon you is like looking at one of Pharaoh's finest horses— a strong, regal steed, pulling His royal chariot. – Song of Solomon 1:9, TPT

After the Lord spoke that scripture to me, I did my research. What I found out was, that during the time of the pharaohs, they would send their servants throughout the known land in search of immature ponies. Then... after submitting them through *intense* training and discipline, they were eventually harnessed to the chariot of pharaoh to usher him into glory during victory parades. Thus, my husband Jeff and I formed "Dappled Horse Ministries"; *Harnessed to the Chariot of the King of Kings.* What has God placed in your heart? I pray that the following encourages you.

God, upon learning to trust us with little, will stretch out our tent pegs and enlarge our territory of influence. Zechariah 4:10 says, *Do not despise small beginnings.* Jesus also says in Luke 16:10, *He who is faithful in what is least is faithful also in much.* That scripture is about money, but it can be applied to all areas of our lives.

Do you feel stuck or frustrated right now as you wait on the Lord? My encouragement to you is to rejoice in small beginnings. We must prove our faithfulness in the little things for Him to promote us. After all, if He could use someone like me, He can use you to be a world-changer! This is His word to you about small beginnings:

Bulbs in the Ground

My child…

Stay close to Me as your next breath,

for I will keep thee in perfect peace.

You will glorify My name.

You will give honor to My name.

Reap what you sow, into a garden that hasn't grown yet.

For they are bulbs in the ground,

and they WILL manifest their beauty in due season.

~Your Way Maker; Christ the Lord~

JOINT CHIEFS OF STAFF

The Lord said to me one day, "Joint Chiefs of Staff." Now that was an awesome word! He was confirming to me that Jeff and I were being jointly called together in ministry to shepherd His sheep. Shepherds have staffs, thus joint chiefs "of staff." Remember, a cord of 3 strands is not easily broken. With Jesus in the center of our lives, we knew we could do anything that He had called us to do, and so can you!

In the meantime, worship Him in spirit and in truth. Are you waiting on a promise from the Lord? All of His promises are yes and amen, right? Sometimes we have to press in even harder, by standing and believing for what He has said will come to pass. Here is what He is saying to you right now:

Good Things Come to Those That Wait

In the coming days, I've arranged something special

to happen to you.

You will see that I reward those

who worship Me in spirit and in truth.

You are my worshiping warrior!

You will see shortly, that I'm going to raise you up

to a level you've never been before.

(New Heights)

Good things come to those that wait, My child.

~Abba Father~

A FLOCK AND A FIELD

After Dappled Horse Ministries was born, something special happened. I attended a meeting where several advertising sales-men were trying to sell radio ads to me at a hair restoration center where I worked. Because we did hair restoration (for those who suffered hair loss due to chemo or hormonal reasons), I respectfully declined. Due to the nature of what we did, we needed to advertise in a medium such as television and print media, so we could show *before and after* photos.

About 10 minutes after they left, there was a knock at my office door. One of the men had come back and he said to me, "I have no idea why I came back, but I felt led to tell you that you have a great

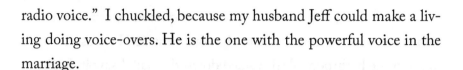

radio voice." I chuckled, because my husband Jeff could make a living doing voice-overs. He is the one with the powerful voice in the marriage.

Nevertheless, as the day went on, I had the unction that the Lord was going to give us a radio show. It grew and grew until I could hardly stand it. I came home filled with expectation. I told Jeff and he looked at me like I was "coo coo for cocoa puffs." Two weeks later as I was waking up, I had a vision. It was of an old-fashioned radio. The Lord spoke and said; *"I'm giving you a flock and a field."* I jumped out of bed, yelling, " I knew it! I knew it!"

Several months later, the Lord said; *"I'm going to open a door that I want you to walk through."*

Two days later I received a call from Paul Ridgeway, and he sounded desperate. He was the lead radio personality on "AM 980, The Mission; Twin Cities Christian Voice." Gladly we said yes to being a last-minute guest on his show. We did not have a clue that this was the new door God wanted us to walk through, because we had been a guest on Paul's show several times in the past. But God! The Word says:

> Behold, I am doing a new thing! Now it springs forth; do you not perceive and know it and will you not give heed to it? I will even make a way in the wilderness and rivers in the desert. – Isaiah 43:19

After we were done, we came out of the recording studio. The Station's Ministry Director, Gary Borgendale, was waiting for us to shake our hands. He asked us if we had ever considered having our own show. Jeff and I smiled at each other and said we would pray about it. We wanted to make sure that the time was right for us to do it. One thing led to another, and they offered us our own show. When we went to their office to sign our contract, I excused myself to go to the bathroom. As I walked down the hall, I saw it. Right in front of me was the old-fashioned radio that I had seen in my vision!

Friend of God, has the Lord revealed to you your unique calling? Remember; it is something only you can do. He does not always give you a vision of the "cover of the jig-saw puzzle box," as He did for me with the radio vision. I saw the *cover,* and then all of the pieces of the puzzle came together. Mostly though, Jesus, The Bread of Life, drops bread crumbs for us to follow. Look for the breadcrumbs! The author and finisher of your faith is calling you into your destiny!

Destiny Day

My precious one… it's destiny day.
Seek ye a harvest from your threshing floor.
For everything I've designed for you
will come to pass in its season.
Recompense in monumental proportion will flood you,
and you will be amazed at My goodness!
No more ransacking by the enemy of your soul,
for I will annihilate him like dust blowing in the wind.
Relegate thoughts of an impoverished mind.
My throne room beckons you.
Press in to Me,
for your destiny will most assuredly come to pass.

~Son of the Living God~

TRAINING FOR REIGNING

Jeff and I went on the air in 2015 with our show "Training for Reigning." What an amazing ride it was. Jeff used to say "Giddy-up" on the air all the time, as it played on our horse theme. But when you think about it, the enemy does not want us to giddy-up. He wants us to put off things in our daily lives and procrastinate. Sometimes he uses the fear of failure to do it. Jesus says,

I am the vine, you are the branches. He who abides in Me, and I in him, bears much fruit; for without Me you can do nothing. – John 15:5, NKJV

Beloved, when you make Jesus your partner in life, YOU CANNOT FAIL. He is waiting for you to invite Him into every area of your life.

One night after starting our show, I was lying in bed trying to fall asleep, when I had a repeat vision of what I saw in 2012. All of a sudden it was as though I left my body and was hovering on the ceiling looking down at Jeff and me in bed.

I then saw a raven swoop in and land in-between us and perch there. He was once again showing me how He had called Elijah to the Brook Cherith. God had arranged for the ravens to fly in bread and meat twice a day to provide for him. This vision was to reassure us that God would supernaturally bring provision to fund the show.

Then the word of the Lord came to him, saying, "Get away from here and turn eastward, and hide by the Brook Cherith, which flows into the Jordan. And it will be that you shall drink from the brook, and I have commanded the ravens to feed you there." So he went and did according to the word of the Lord, for he went and stayed by the Brook Cherith, which flows into the Jordan. The ravens brought him bread and meat in the morning, and bread and meat in the evening; and he drank from the brook . –1 Kings 17:2-6

The Word calls the Lord *Jehovah-Jireh,* which means "The Lord My Provider." For almost three years, He provided financially for Jeff and me to have a radio show on the sixteenth largest Christian talk radio station in the country. By August 2017, though, we had to put the contract payment on our credit card. We thought, *What does this mean?* Then I was shown the following in the Word;

And it happened after a while… that the brook dried up, because there had been no rain in the land.

Yep, the radio brook had dried up for us and we had to suspend the show. I could not understand it! But then I realized that God had STILL sent Elijah there, albeit for a season. This made me feel so much better. I was eager to see what God had for us in the next season in our lives. On to Zarapeth!

Are you ready to have the Lord move you into your destiny?

Explosive Revelation and Increase

Precious child…

Farther down the road,

you will receive explosive divine revelation and increase.

All you can see right now is the road in front of you.

Be of good cheer fearless one…

for I have overcome the world.

You will see My great strength towards you

in the coming days.

Ratchet up your faith…

For a hope-filled heart

is the catalyst that moves you towards your destiny.

~Christ the King~

Chapter 14

THE COOL OF THE DAY

And they were both naked, the man and his wife, and were not ashamed. – **Genesis 2:25 NKJV**

YOUR FIG LEAVES ARE GONE

One day the Lord said to me, *"Daughter, your fig leaves are gone!"* I thought, *Of course they are.* He then asked me this question; *"Why then do you try to hide from Me sometimes?"* Ouch! I had no idea I ever did that. Wow. That was an arrow that zinged straight to my heart.

Beloved, when we have a full revelation of the finished work of Jesus on the cross, we can walk with the Father in the cool of the day as Adam and Eve did. They were clothed with the glory of God, and they were not ashamed. They were not ashamed that is, until they sinned.

Then the eyes of both of them were opened, and they knew that they were naked; and they sewed fig leaves together and made themselves coverings. And they heard the sound of the Lord God walking in the garden in the cool of the day, and Adam and his wife hid themselves from the presence of the Lord God among the trees of the garden. Then the Lord God called to Adam and said to him, "Where are you?" — Genesis 3:7-9, NKJV

Basically, the Lord was saying to me that I was allowing the devil to bring me shame and condemnation over sin in my life. Friend of God, it is crucial that we get a revelation that Jesus already shed blood for every sin we have ever committed, past, present and future. He sees us as righteous, because *Jesus* is righteous and lives on the inside of us.

The only way the devil can get an inroad into our lives is when we come into agreement with his lies. We can walk with our Heavenly Father in the cool of the day. When Jesus yelled out on the cross; "IT IS FINISHED!" it was done. The veil was torn, and we could now go directly to the Father without having to go through a priest. The second we became born again, the fig leaves that covered the shame of our sin were completely removed. Halleluiah!

It doesn't mean, though, that we can go on and not be accountable to the cross. Repentance is a gift, and it is a lifestyle. When we do sin, it is amazing that we can come back into complete intimacy with the Father when we repent. Nothing can separate us from His love! Precious one… He desires to walk with you in the cool of the day!

Cool of the Day

The Father wants you to walk beside Him
in the cool of the day.

The reparations and the repair job that you have believed for
will arrive soon.

I will see to it that every arrangement that needs to be made
for you to fulfill your destiny, will come to pass.

Your Risen King is on it! Your Risen King proclaims it!
My desires are your desires!

~Resurrected King~

PERPETUAL OIL

What an amazing blood covenant we have with the Lord! Not only does He cast our sins as far as the east is to the west, but He sends us Holy Spirit to be our comforter, helper, and spiritual truth guide. He guides us into ALL truth. I love how He opens up the Word of God to us. He is the revealer of Jesus, our Lord. Oh, how I love Him so! Jesus says to us;

When He, the Spirit of truth, has come, He will guide you into all truth; for He will not speak on His own authority, but whatever He hears He will speak; and He will tell you things to come. He will glorify Me, for He will take of

165

what is Mine and declare it to you. All things that the Father has are Mine. Therefore, I said that He will take of Mine and declare it to you. – John 16:13-15, NKJV

I encourage you to seek a relationship with Holy Spirit. He is the one who reveals Jesus. You cannot get a revelation of the Word / Jesus without Him. The word says that *spirit discerns spirit*. He is also the One who gives us spiritual gifts.

There are diversities of gifts, but the same Spirit. There are differences of ministries, but the same Lord. And there are diversities of activities, but it is the same God who works all in all. But the manifestation of the Spirit is given to each one for the profit of all. – Corinthians 12:4-7, NKJV

Those who know me know that my biggest pet peeve is cessationisim. This is the belief that the *gifts of Holy Spirit died with the last apostle*. Paul wrote 1 Corinthians to the church regarding spiritual gifts. He did not write and say; *these gifts are only for the twelve apostles until they die*. Deception renders powerless those who believe this. He sent Holy Spirit to form a powerful church filled with miracles, signs, and wonders. Jesus said….

Most assuredly, I say to you, he who believes in Me, the works that I do he will do also; and greater works than these he will do, because I go to My Father. – John 14:12, NKJV

Also, anyone who blasphemes the Holy Spirit by attributing His works to the devil is committing the unpardonable sin. Jesus says you can blaspheme the Son of Man and be forgiven, (because salvation is open to all until they die). But when He discussed blaspheming Holy Spirit, He was talking to the Pharisees who claimed He had his cast out a demon by the power of Beelzebub.

And the scribes who came down from Jerusalem said, "He has Beelzebub," and, "By the ruler of the demons He casts out demons." So He called them to Himself and said to them in parables: "How can Satan cast out Satan? If a kingdom is divided against itself, that kingdom cannot stand. And if a house is divided against itself, that house cannot stand. And if Satan has risen up against himself, and is divided, he cannot stand, but has an end. No one can enter a strong man's house and plunder his goods, unless he first binds the strong man. And then he will plunder his house.

"Assuredly, I say to you, all sins will be forgiven the sons of men, and whatever blasphemies they may utter; but he who blasphemes against the Holy Spirit never has forgiveness, but is subject to eternal condemnation"— because they said, "He has an unclean spirit." –Mark 3:22-28, NKJV

The Bride cannot operate without the gifts. Jesus said to cast out demons, heal the sick, and to raise the dead. How could we possibly function in those commands without Holy Spirit?

Paul writes that we should earnestly desire the best gifts. Amen!

But earnestly desire the best gifts, and yet I show you a more excellent way. – 1 Corinthians 12:31, NKJV

If you are not yet Spirit-filled, I encourage you to ask Jesus right now, to baptize you with the Holy Spirit.

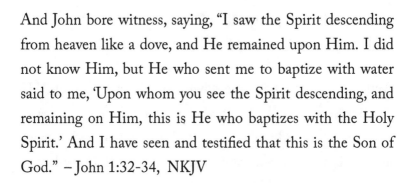

And John bore witness, saying, "I saw the Spirit descending from heaven like a dove, and He remained upon Him. I did not know Him, but He who sent me to baptize with water said to me, 'Upon whom you see the Spirit descending, and remaining on Him, this is He who baptizes with the Holy Spirit.' And I have seen and testified that this is the Son of God." – John 1:32-34, NKJV

The Lord is inviting you to a new level of intimacy with Holy Spirit. Are you sensitive to Him? Remember the story of "The Princess and the Pea?" It is a tale about royal sensitivity by Hans Christian Anderson. The story tells of a prince who wants to marry a princess but is having difficulty finding a suitable wife. Something is always wrong with those he meets. He cannot be certain they are *real* princesses, because they either have bad table manners, are too fat or thin or not beautiful.

One stormy night, a young woman drenched with rain seeks shelter in the prince's castle. She claims to be a princess, so the prince's mother decides to test their unexpected and unwitting guest by placing a pea in the bed she is offered for the night. It is covered by twenty mattresses and twenty feather-beds. In the morning, the guest tells her hosts that she endured a sleepless night, kept awake by something hard in the bed that she is certain has bruised her. The prince rejoices. Only a real princess would have the sensitivity to feel a pea through such a quantity of bedding, so the two are married.

The Princess and the Pea
Sensitivity Training for Royalty

The Lord said…quick decisions will need

to be made on the battlefield.

You will hear My voice saying…

"This is the way, walk in it.

You do not live by bread alone, but by My every word

I speak to you about your destiny.

I will show you hidden things to come."

~Spirit of the Living God~

A RIVER RUNS THROUGH IT

The Word says that out of our bellies (Heart) shall flow Rivers of Living Water. I Love that! You can bring life to people's days because the Living Water (Jesus) flows out of you and splashes on everyone you interact with. One day, Holy Spirit gave me a vision of a poster that said; *"Just Drink the Water!"* Is your tank full of Living Water? Fill up, splash and soak in the Living Water and you will spill out onto others.

THE NARROW PATH

Enter by the narrow gate; for wide is the gate and broad is the way that leads to destruction, and there are many who go in by it. Because narrow is the gate and difficult is the way which leads to life, and there are few who find it.

–Matthew 7:13-14, NKJV

It seems the longer I walk down the Highway of Holiness, the narrower the path gets. The Highway of Holiness, my friends, should be a one-way street, with no turning back and no round-abouts. Things I could get by with years ago, I cannot do today. For example, there are certain television shows I used to watch that I would not dream of watching today. We are to keep our eye-gate pure, says the Lord.

> The lamp of the body is the eye. If therefore your eye is good, your whole body will be full of light. But if your eye is bad, your whole body will be full of darkness. If therefore the light that is in you is darkness, how great is that darkness!
>
> – Matthew 6:22-23, NKJV

Jeff and I used to say on the radio all the time; "Whatever you watch on television, you are inviting those spirits into your home." I am appalled at some of the shows on TV today, with their sex, language, and violence. Parents especially need to be careful of what they watch with their kids. People can get numb to what they see, and that is extremely dangerous.

THIS ONE THING

On June 13th, 2017 I was taken to Heaven. For years, I begged to come up to the Throne Room as I worshipped Him in spirit and in truth, then I had the revelation that I was asking the wrong thing. One night Jeff and I were watching "It's Supernatural "with Sid Roth and he had a guest who was talking about when Peter walked on water. I almost jumped out of my chair! Peter just didn't walk on water, he was able to do so, because Jesus *commanded* Peter to come to Him.

Starting the next morning in my prayer closet, my request became a demand. I no longer asked if He would bring me up to the Throne Room. I yelled out, "Jesus, COMMAND me to come to You!" Five days was all it took. On June 13th, 2017 in the middle of the night I was taken to Heaven. I found myself to be in a room without walls, that seemed to go on into infinity.

I was surrounded by the most intense bluish-white light that would blind a person in the natural. The Lord came in and He said only two words. He said, *"Psalm 27."* The only way I can describe it, was that I *literally became* that Psalm because the Giver of Life breathed it into me.

I knew why He spoke it to me.

Here's the one thing I crave from God, the one thing I seek above all else: I want the privilege of living with him every moment in his house, finding the sweet loveliness of His face, filled with awe, delighting in his glory and grace. I want to live my life so close to Him that He takes pleasure in my every prayer. Lord, when you said to me, "Seek my face," my inner being responded, "I'm seeking your face with all my heart."

– Psalm 27:4, 8, TPT

Beloved, I had a literal encounter with the Word and He wants you to have an encounter too! Ask Him to bring you a hunger for the Living Bread. He will do so and open up to revelation to your heart beyond measure.

BRIDE OF THE MOUNTAIN

Friend of God, we are coming to the close of my testimony part of the book. I do want you to know that Jesus beckons you to come up the mountain with Him. It is an invitation to enter in to a union *so intimate* with your Bridegroom King, that it will leave you breathless.

I would encourage you to read the entire book of "Song of Solomon," preferably in *The Passion Translation*, to experience the kind of love He is inviting you to receive. Along with your climb, though, comes refining through trials that are designed to purge you of your dross. These trials are an act of love, designed so that you can shine like gold. Are you ready to say, "I surrender to you Jesus, no matter what the cost?" Join me in confessing this out loud...

Bride of the Mountain

I've made up my mind.
Until the darkness disappears and the dawn has fully come,
in spite of shadows and fears,
I will go to the mountaintop with You—
the mountain of suffering love and the hill of burning incense.
Yes, I will be Your bride.
As Bride of the Mountain,
I will climb with You to the highest peaks.
I will enter through Your Archway of Trust.
I am undone by Your love, my Beloved.

(Song of Solomon; 4:6, 8; TPT)

I have aptly named the last section of the book "The Heartbeat of Heaven; Love Declarations from the Father's Heart." The Lord told me that all of the words I have collected in my binders contain the Heartbeat of Heaven. I pray that upon reading these beautiful utterances from Him, that you will receive them as your own. Take time to meditate on them, as they were spoken FOR YOU!

I love you, my reader. It is no accident that this book is in your hands right now. I pray for God's highest and best for you moving forward. Until we meet in Heaven… I bid you adieu.

All my love towards you,

MB

Love Declarations from the Father's Heart

Decrees of Intimacy and Love

Your Destiny Awaits

The Warrior in You

Realms of Heaven

Decrees of Intimacy and Love

I Beseech Your Beauty

Faithful one...I beseech your beauty.

When you and I are alone together...

magnificent things transpire in the glory realm.

Feel My loving arms pull you into the shelter of My wings.

You are My treasure. You are My joy!

Your King greatly desires your beauty, your purity,

and your holiness.

You are set aside for royal purposes.

Relish in My care and bask in My love.

Jehovah Kabod; King of Glory

Definition of beseech: To invoke, crave or to call upon

Wild at Heart

Precious child of Mine…

Signs and wonders shall follow you wherever you go.

Glory, Glory, and more Glory!

Be wild at heart! Be sound of mind!

Be quick to obey!

There is rectitude in servitude.

You are fiercely loved!

Your Abba

Forward March

Forward march, beautiful one!

I desire thee and I long for thee in the cool of the day.

You are My faithful warrior, and I will guide thee

and make sure that thou are covered and protected.

Say to yourself …

THIS is the day the Lord has made…

I will rejoice and be glad in it!

Follow Me to the harvest fields for they

are white and ready.

Peace be still, My child.

Now… let us make beautiful music together!

Your Bridegroom King

Savoir Faire

*I breathlessly wait for you to get up in the morning
to seek My presence.*

Upon your arrival into the womb of the morning…

*I stand with outstretched arms to greet you with a sacrificial love.
I bled so that you could have fellowship with the Father.*

The veil was torn, My Little Dwelling...

So that you could be ushered into My Throne Room

*The beauty of My Holiness surrounds you!
Awake, Awake My beauty…*

*You carry My Light wherever you go.
For I have given you Savoir Faire.
And you shall thrive beyond measure.*

Your Bridegroom King decrees this.

Savoir Faire definition…

Poise, grace, style and accomplishment

Perpetual Praise

Your perpetual praise is significant to Me.

Continue to seek Me in the secret place for
Your sweet aroma delights My senses.

For I will do for you something so amazing…
that you would not believe it if it were told you.
(Habakkuk 1:5)

Your praise gallery in Heaven is stunning!

Watch me work in your life as you are catapulted into
the realm of the Spirit!

You are My chosen vessel.

I have anointed you with dunamous power.
Give glory to My name!

Your King has spoken

Fierce Intimacy

Mandrakes… mandrakes, My chosen one.
Eat the fruit of My love and I will pour out a blessing upon you.

Seek Me fiercely! Love Me utterly!
Consecrate your life to Me; your Daddy…
My sweet, sweet child.

I will whisk you away in the night to receive divinely inspired
utterance from My lips to yours.

Kisses from Heaven rain down on you My precious one.

The veil has been torn.
Enter into the throne room fearless!
Anointed with sacred oil,

I smell your sacrifice… and it is pleasing to Me

(Mandrakes are the Hebrew fruit of love)

Dwelling Together

Blood-bought child… pay attention to what I'm telling you.

There is coming a breakthrough in your life of huge proportions.

There is a revelation of great magnitude coming to you.

So much so… that it will cause others to seek Me in awe.

Taste and see that I AM good!

Seek me with every fiber of your being and I will be found.

For I am in you and you are in Me…

and we dwell together in the Father.

Radiant Bride

Radiant Bride…

Come to Me in a field of white lilies.

For I've produced a royal banquet in your honor.

(Decree)

Lord, imprint Your beauty upon my life…

spirit soul and body.

Thank you, Lord, for causing the lights

to go on in my heart.

Thank You for putting the pieces of my life together

with understanding and hope.

(Lilies are symbols of purity in the temple
of our inner being)

Accouterments of Heaven

Reap a harvest where you faint not!
For I will deliver thee and I will honor thee
through the trials of life.
Bask in the glory of My presence.
My countenance shines upon you…
for it is as bright as the noonday,
My little lamb.
My sheep know My voice.
It is My pleasure to give you the Kingdom
and all the accouterments of Heaven.

Your Lord God has spoken.

Rewards from God's Bounty

To the anointed one I have chosen…

Reap a harvest where you have not sown.

Relinquish thoughts of doubt about future

callings and commissions.

Bear up, be strong, don't give up, don't give in!

Rewards from My bounty will be brought forth into the light.

For they will transcend time and be

deposited into your life.

I've decreed it!

Jesus; King of the World

Your Destiny Awaits

Explosive Revelation and Increase

Adored child of Mine…

Farther down the road you will receive explosive

divine revelation and increase.

All you can see right now is the road in front of you,

but be of good cheer…

for I have overcome the world.

You will see My great strength towards you

in the coming days.

Ratchet up your faith…

For a hope-filled heart is the catalyst that moves

you towards your destiny.

Christ the King

Promises Do Come True

Marvelous things await you My anointed one.

Forward March!

Sing to Me a new song… for it is a new day for you!

Move over and let Me take the wheel,

for I am about to steer you in a new direction.

You will see things in a new way

and you will see things clearer than you ever have before.

For the Promise Keeper is keeping His promises

towards you.

Watch them unfold before your very eyes.

Dream on, dreamer!

Your Heavenly Dream Giver.

By faith Sarah herself also received strength
to conceive seed, and she bore a child when
she was past the age, because she judged Him
faithful who had promised.

Hebrews 11:11

Divine Destiny

Your destiny is calling you, beloved.

For surging within you is the River of Life.

More will be revealed in the coming days.

In the meantime… carry on, soldier!

Dive into the deep things that await you in My holy Word.

Being catapulted to your divine destiny is as

sure as the light of day!

My grace covers you.

Lord of Lords

Pret a Porter

Hang on fearless one, you're almost there!

I will keep you hidden until the appropriate time.

Watch Me pluck you out of your current circumstances

and plant you like a rose in My garden.

Your grass is about to grow.

The frost will melt and the lilies will bud.

For the land which I'm sending you,

will become a luscious garden.

You've been pulled and tested for I am equipping

you for service

You are My Prêt a Porter.

Creator God

Prêt a Porter definition…

A Designer's Ready-to-Wear Collection

The Abundance of Rain

My faithful one,…you have felt the abundance of rain.

And there have been times the enemy has tried

to trick you and lie to you.

But you have held fast to my word and been faithful,

during times of great sorrow.

Therefore…I am giving you the opportunity of a lifetime!

I will catapult you into the realm of the Spirit.

For the day will come soon…

That I will manifest My glory in you and through you.

Taste and see that I am good!

Get ready for an abundance of rain, My precious!

Your Heavenly Rainmaker

Doubt and Unbelief Shattered

Challenge yourself in matters of the heart, My love.

Resolve them by coming to Me.

Rearrange your life to spend more time

with Me in the sheepfold.

There is a bountiful harvest of blessings

too numerous to count that awaits you.

Allow Me to purify your conscience from insecurities,

doubt, and unbelief

towards your capabilities and your calling.

My manifest presence surrounds you.

Swing wide the gate of your heart!

Carry yourself with dignity always.

Your King has spoken.

Servitude

It is from a place of servitude that I will catapult

you to your destiny.

Many are called; few are chosen.

You are My indentured servant who is willing to forsake all to

serve Me in the days ahead.

Throw caution to the wind, My Little Dwelling…

for I will be there to catch you if you fall.

Pour out yourself on the Rock!

Make the choice to come quickly when called!

Minuscule opportunities turn into great,

vast and rich territories.

Indentured Servant definition…
"One who is subservient to, and entirely at the
disposal of his master"

He Is Pleased with You

My beloved…

I am so pleased with whom you have become.

Every breath you take… I joyously give you.

Every step you take… I am with you.

Every need you have… I fill.

Every vow you make… I receive.

Every curse that tries to touch you… I will destroy!

Lord of Heaven

Destiny Day

My beautiful child…
It's destiny day!
Seek ye a harvest from your threshing floor.
For everything I've designed for you will come to pass
in its season.
Recompense in monumental proportion will flood you
and you will be amazed at My goodness!
No more ransacking by the enemy of your soul, for
I will annihilate him like dust blowing in the wind.
Relegate thoughts of an impoverished mind.
I will guide thee to the steps of My altar.
My throne room beckons you, My precious.

Son of the Living God

The Latch Key

Search your heart and mind for answers to the calling

I have placed on your life.

Are you satisfied with the mundane?

Are you glorified in My name?

Then watch, wait, pray, and seek.

For then you shall find the key to a latch.

A latchkey to a destiny far beyond what

you can comprehend.

Turn the key into the lock that's been waiting for you

before the foundation of time.

Now get going and seek the key, My chosen one.

Messiah Jesus; the One who calls you.

The Warrior in You

Fearsome and Noisome to the Enemy

Fearless one…

I love you and I ravish you with My love.

You have been bought with a price!

There is nothing I can't heal, change, or subdue within you.

You are jeweled, and I encase you in My Glory.

You are doused with the fragrance of Heaven.

You are fearsome and noisome to the enemy.

Branded in purity and truth are you…

You have My seal of approval.

Jehovah Kabod; King of Glory

Fearsome = Frightening, especially in appearance

Noisome = Disagreeable and unpleasant, foul smelling

No Fear of Man

Drink deeply of Me and receive an impartation

of holiness and purity.

Move swiftly into areas of forgiveness!

Rectitude, My child… rectitude!

For I will keep thee in perfect peace.

My Spirit will reign mightily in your life.

Do not fear man.

Do not fear challenges.

For they are out there…

To arm you with strength

and to sharpen your skills for battle.

Soak in My mercy.

Rectitude definition… A morally upright walk

Prepare Your Heart

Favored one…

The time has come for Me to show you
great and mighty things you did not know.
Prepare your heart to receive these downloads,
for all must come to pass for My plan in the earth.
Times will be difficult in the days ahead…
but you will forge mightily through, because
you are more than a conqueror!
I will make a way for you to prosper
and you will fight the good fight of faith!
I am there to receive you and all of your requests…
large or small.
You will be triumphant and mighty in battle!
I will never leave you or forsake you.
Remember My goodness in the days ahead.

Faithful Father

War Horse

Your heart has been transformed.

You are a war horse and the

fragrance of your beauty ascends to Heaven.

You have piqued My interest, redeemed one.

I intently gaze upon your every move.

You are special to Me!

So much so...

That I roar My love over you!

No Failure with God

*There will be no failure to complete any mission
that I give you.
Failure is unacceptable to a war hero.
Keep yourself exposed and vulnerable to the
things of the Spirit.
Rest assured….
I, the Lord of the Dance;
will accompany you towards the end result.
Make no mistake about it!
My ability to deliver you from the enemy surpasses all knowledge
that you would entertain with your natural mind.
Realms of the angelic surround you.
Be not afraid, soldier, for you are steeped in authority!
Be quick to obey.*

Christ Jesus

The Heart of a Warrior

There will come a time where you will reap a harvest
where you have not sown.
You have embedded in you…
wisdom, knowledge, and the heart of a warrior.
I will keep thee in perfect peace as you go into battle.
Trust Me utterly and completely.
You will dwell with me in the King's Forest.
For I will bring thee to the River Ahava, to drink from the
fountain of Living Water.
Let your speech be always with grace and
seasoned with salt.

Lord of Hosts

(Ahava is the Hebrew word for love)

Defeating Jabin

*Justice, fortitude, and the countenance of My Son are in
the order of My days for you.*

Reap My goodness…

For you have sown love and mercy to those who needed it.

Attributes of My glory shine through you!

*I will keep thee in perfect peace through the rigors of life,
so relegate thoughts of an impoverished mind.*

Sanctified, purified, and ready to do battle are you.

*Side-by-side we will defeat Jabin, the oppressor;
on the battlefield.*

*For I will send a torrential downpour and he will be dragged
into the mud with his chariots and his minions!*

Yes… pulled down by My mighty hand!

This is the way, walk in it.

Captain of the Hosts

Nickelback

I have earmarked you for greatness!

You are victorious in Me.

The anointing is strong to carry you through whatever

I ask you to do.

You are bathed in the Oil of Authority.

Do not serve the devil a tasty dish, because

he wants your mind.

Take every thought captive that exalts itself

against the knowledge of Me.

Focus on My goodness and overcome his penny ante tricks.

Penny ante definition… small time- 2-bit tricks

A Nickelback is a safety in football

War Hero

Chosen one…

Get ready to be plunged into the deep!

For I will pull you into the depths of My ocean…

The ocean of love, grace and mercy.

Mysteries, power and provision are yours for the taking.

I am decorating you as a war hero.

And may you have the power to understand, as all
God's people should, how wide, how long, how high,
and how deep his love is.

Ephesians 3:18

Redemption Is Mine

Redemption is Mine saith the Lord!

Years of hardship...

Years of squalor...

Years of chaos...

Years of unfruitfulness...

ALL these shall be restored to you.

For the thief has been found and he must repay seven-fold.

For I will make a way where there seems to be no way.

You shall see your life unfolding

in extravagance and love.

Master of the Universe

Realms of Heaven

Dancing with Jesus

I will catch you away to the throne room, My little one.

Come dance the night away with Me and you will discover

the covering and the mantle that I've chosen for you.

Capture My love as it cascades down from Heaven.

Multitudes will come to know My glory through the

words I give you to speak.

Come dine with Me in Heaven.

Rewards will be given to you in the secret place.

Your Master Decrees it

Precious to God

Beloved... I crave your company!

You are beautiful and stunning...

robed in a gown of gold.

Your time with Me is more precious to Me

than the cattle on a thousand hills.

Reparations are coming!

Be still and know that I AM God.

Drink deeply of Me.

Speak softly of Me.

Speak loudly of Me.

Whispers in the night will come to you saying

This is the way... walk in it.

I love you with an everlasting love,

My holy and precious one!

Abba

Whispers in the Night

Hear Me softly, for whispers in the night

and daydreams in the day.

Dreams and desires carefully chosen by your

Papa given to you.

When you abide in My presence…

The wellspring of your life flows

from the Living Water in

the Throne Room.

There is majesty in Providence.

You will be catapulted in the realm of the Spirit

and you will be amazed at My goodness!

You are fearless and bathed in the oil of authority…

Ready for battle.

Seek My face.

Pay the price.

A Fruitful Endeavor

I am Jehovah God!

I am mighty and powerful!

Magnanimous and worthy to receive honor and glory!

I say to the wheat fields: bloom... and they bring forth grain!

I say to the mountains: move… and they move!

You are My chosen one, My child.

For I will raise you up to walk in heavenly places

and it will be a fruitful endeavor.

Watch Me catapult you into the realm of the Spirit.

It shall be done!

The One who Created you

Fiery Stones

My Royal Chariot awaits you,

My dearest darling.

Your ball gown is of fiery stones.

We will dance the night away

And catch a sunrise.

Behold, I will lay your stones with colorful gems, and lay your foundations with sapphires. I will make your pinnacles of rubies, your gates of crystal, and all your walls of precious stones.

Isaiah 54:11-12, NKJV

The Wedding Ceremony

The King of Kings and the Lord of Lords says…

Relish Me… for I AM your Husband.

Cherish Me… your worthy Bridegroom.

The wedding preparations have been made.

Put on your beautiful wedding dress, My beloved…

for your Bridegroom wait anxiously for you at the altar.

Come join your heart with Mine, for our marriage is eternal.

Our marriage is a covenant that cannot be broken.

Just as in a wedding ceremony on earth;
the groom waits "at the altar" for the Bride.
Jesus, our Bridegroom, waits at the altar in Heaven
for us to come to Him.

Golden Ribbons from Heaven

Greater works than these you shall do in My name says your
King. For I go to the Father on your behalf.
And you will do great exploits in My name
and the glory…oh, the glory!
Speak life to the lost and broken-hearted!
For I will take the feeble and the weak-kneed and My glory
shall shine upon them.
People shall taste and see that I am good through you!
Seek a harvest from people's threshing floors.
Take their chaff and cast it into the wind of the Spirit!
Dedicate the remaining grain as an offering to Me.
And I will shower thee with golden ribbons from Heaven.

Out of your innermost being is flowing the fullness
of my Spirit—never failing to satisfy.
Within your womb there is a birthing of harvest wheat; they
are the sons and daughters nurtured
by the purity you impart.

Song of Solomon 7:2-3, TPT

A First Fruits Offering

Blood-bought child, thank Me for what
I'm about to do in your life.
For you've been purchased with a price,
and the glory cloud is over you wherever you go.
An open heaven rains showers of mercy and love on you,
My precious.
Follow the yellow brick road to your great destiny…
for you have overcome by the Blood of the Lamb.
Seek a harvest from your threshing floor and
wave your sheaves before Me.
Your sacrifice pleases Me.

Jehovah Kabod; King of Glory

When you enter the land, I am going to give you and you
reap its harvest; Bring to the priest (Jesus) a sheaf of the first
grain you harvest.

Leviticus 23:9

My Glory Light

The God of the universe beckons you to come up higher.

Let your soul be nourished with MY emotions and MY

extravagant love poured out on you this day.

You are kind, thoughtful and persuasive.

Your extravagant giving comes from your heart

of love for Me.

Fear not, my precious one…

For I will hold your hand through all trauma in this life.

For I will give thee a fountain of revelation

in accordance with My word.

Keep on keeping on.

Keep on pressing in.

For My glory light shines upon thee!

Your Master

Rainbows of Light

My exquisite raiment covers you, My anointed one!

Glistening, dancing, and shining rays from My presence.

Rainbows of light from Heaven above…

Beckoning you to come up higher, into the realms of Me.

Feast on revelation poured out through this Light

Catapulted into the heavenly realm of My Spirit you shall go.

King of Glory

ABOUT THE AUTHOR

MB Busch is the President of Heartbeat of Heaven Ministries and a prophetic voice to the Body of Christ. She is known for her powerful testimony of how she was delivered from a 30-year battle with alcohol, drugs and bulimia. MB preaches that King Jesus can summon anyone out of darkness, and her passion is to set the captives free from any form of bondage and to reveal the love of the Father.

When MB decrees prophetic words from the Father's heart to His children, their spiritual fig leaves fall away. She not only is a firebrand that has preached all over the world through various forms of media, but she ignites people's passion for the Lord on a daily basis.

MB studied through the Bethel Supernatural School of Ministry, Redding, CA and The Patricia King Institute. She holds an Honorary Doctorate of Christian Ministry from Dayspring Theological University. She is married to Jeff and both are certified inner-healing and deliverance counselors through Elijah House.

Currently, they serve as Altar Ministers at Living Word Christian Center. MB is ordained though Patricia King's Women in Ministry Network (WIMN), where she serves in a regional leadership capacity.

MB, Jeff and their family dog, Chloe, make their home in Minneapolis MN.

CPSIA information can be obtained
at www.ICGtesting.com
Printed in the USA
LVHW052352180122
708648LV00012B/814

9 780578 500003